AF240875

DEBT SLAVERY

Max Milo Éditions, Paris, 2023
www.maxmilo.com
ISBN : 978-2-315-01257-2

Jean-Clet Martin

DEBT SLAVERY

Max Milo
ESSAIS-DOCUMENTS

"Man is no longer the locked-in man, but the indebted man.
It's true that capitalism has kept as a constant the extreme
misery of three-quarters of humanity, too poor for debt,
too numerous for confinement: control will have to face
not only the dissipation of borders, but the explosions of
shantytowns and ghettos."

Gilles Deleuze, *Pourparlers*, p. 246.

INTRODUCTION

That philosophy should have something to say about economic processes should come as no surprise to anyone who, as a reader of Nietzsche or Marx, understands that money is not matter. The way money circulates is a matter of *dematerialization*, of an increasingly ethereal ideality. Which sometimes gives us the feeling that we're swimming in bad metaphysics. In Book I of *Politics*, Aristotle already considered money to be a fictitious, unreal genre. Money never derives its value from itself. It is a sign, a *symbol*: it takes the place of what it represents, replacing a very abstract value with an artificial image[1]. Its purpose is not to be kept, and it serves no purpose in itself. It only makes sense to be exchanged, to be sold. And because it is not a thing but a print, an imprint[2], its acquisition occupies no space, belongs to no place. Unencumbered, it carries the risk, as Aristotle pointed out in reference to Solon's statement, of

---

1. Aristotle, *History of Animals*, I, 6, 491 a 20.
2. *Id.*, *Politics*, I, 9, 1257 a 40, trans. J. Tricot, Paris, Vrin, 1962.

going beyond all limits. Its ideality meets no obstacle, and its storage poses no problem of space. It can therefore take an *unlimited* turn[3] for data banks. It is boundless, and lends itself to excess, since it weighs virtually nothing, is filled with nothing, and holds no place of its own, as is the case with *physical* things. It is a number without weight, because it is printed. It is first inscribed on metal as an abstract stamp, an engraving that even lightens it, producing tenuous signs before multiplying into banknotes, cheques and digital data. Metal as much as paper is only the medium of a volatile trace, a belief, the circulation of a metaphor destined for exchange. Conversely, by virtue of its volume, a massive object cannot be exchanged, cannot occupy the place of another, nor can a house be placed on an already-occupied lot or taken with it. The real is always very cumbersome. Money, on the other hand, has no smell, as the saying goes, meaning that we can't really locate it or account for its provenance, that it can always be laundered, that it's neutral from the moment it's printed. It can be exchanged on increasingly thin supports, as virtual as the wind.

The digitization of transactions today leads us to believe that there is no longer any financial substance, no *materialism* in the current course of values. We have entered the realm of highly ethereal flows, of bankcards, of computerized, digital transactions, whose encryption is no longer evaluated in terms of human duration. It's a temporality that is only accessible to computer measurement. Behind this network lies a

---

3. *Id, ibid,* I, 8, 1256, b 35.

veritable artificial paradise, a "city of God" that philosophy understands better than the laws of economics, an economy that Marx dreamed of overthrowing, of resting on the feet of real, material production. The laws of economics, in fact, give precedence to finalities as abstract, as miraculous as the promise of happiness, of the prestige traditionally embodied in what must be called a "metaphysics", a region said to be "beyond palpable physics". By imposing such a paradise, and at the same time creating hell in the zones of production, global governance and its economy cannot be understood without a philosophical approach, if only to denounce the speculative god embodied by money, and announce its imminent death.

First and foremost, we owe to Rousseau the certainty that there is no god in the order of human affairs. There is no god to justify a sovereignty based solely on *convention*. And conventions, if they are to be respected and followed when there is no external basis for them, must possess a force of conviction yet to be invented, yet to be discovered. Without God to back up the bill, an *agreement* is needed that commits both parties. And we always agree on the value of money when we make an exchange, when we establish a bargain, a market. We never have any doubts about the effectiveness of the exchange guaranteed by honor-based bargaining. Hence the modern idea of a politics of *contract*, binding free individuals under the sovereignty of a democratic state[4]. But

---

4. This philosophical adventure is that of the *Social Contract*, the forbidden book that made Rousseau the public enemy of monarchical Europe.

what is such a contract worth? How can we justify its strength of conviction and its own faith?

Nietzsche, another philosopher, came up with the idea that submission is never deliberate. This very special contract, this social contract by which we bow to an authority without complaint, contains a very strange element of faith. A spiritual alienation that leads to free submission, a rather curious inner constraint in which we ourselves agree to lose all our rights. It's out of *duty* that we submit to a moral authority, before being political. How does such a duty work in the economic sphere? Capitalism was certainly born of the exploitation of this form of debt, fault and even *capital sin*. It establishes a relationship between individuals with a very specific *contract*: that of being indebted at will. Every debt is a promise made to another to "owe" him something, to repay him unconditionally. Historically, this was done by pledging one's honor, and sometimes by liquidating highly symbolic family assets[5]. And it is this symbolic part that is untenable, unpayable when this debt was entered into, as is often the case, in the name of an affective model, or even more often in the name of charity. The charity, kindness and benevolence of credit organizations can never be repaid. It's a gift so one-sided that it can only be erased by paying so disproportionately that it makes you as much a slave as you want to be. It's because this is the case, and because economics is bound up with irrational behavior, that we find in it

---

5. Laurent de Sutter analyzes this magical royalty in his book *Magic* (Paris, PUF, 2015), notably in use in Roman law times.

such an unscientific vocabulary of "trust", "effort", "sacrifice" - a vocabulary that characterizes servitude, when there are masters to wrest trust from slaves who apparently return it according to a fee that has become unlimited.

Without debt, contracted under the apparent charity of the wealthiest, there could be no alienation. Bank charity looks so disinterested that it induces a logic of misery, shame and guilt. Those who contract a debt, those who are victims of someone else's charity, agree to enter a vicious circle. He accepts this apparently generous offer, ready to repay such a loan by any means: with his body, with his work, with the use of his children, his possessions... When faced with a loan, it's always a question of being ready, ready for anything, with your feet to the fire. And in this presence[6], it's a question of laying one's life bare for recognition, as Hegel also knew. Debt plays on recognition. It puts us in the position of having to pay in other ways, of being endlessly *grateful* to benefactors. For the weakest, this debt has always already begun, so to speak, before they were born. Debt is a fault, an "original sin" for the newborn, who must repay the contract of his elders, the debt of his close relatives, the reason for which he does not even know. Why can't we break such a contract, which Marx also sees as alienation, a form of slavery?

This is the question that this essay will attempt to answer, by showing how the global financial system plays on a morality that is not strictly economic. It includes a theological

---

6. The word *"prestance"* should be understood here not in its usual sense, but in relation to its etymology, which is similar to that of the word *"prêt"* - he who lends is *prestant* (from the verb *prester*), hence *"prestance"*.

ingredient, owing to a belief in an immaterial paradise that belongs nowhere. It is ecumenical, and claims that everything can be relocated in the name of a god who is no longer just the god of money, which is still too material. The well-off have no need to line their pockets with it. On the contrary, it's the poor who, without a bank account, have to justify their purchases with coins made of metal. The rich, on the other hand, circulate without securities, without having to pay anything: all they have to do is transmit, by satellite, by cell phone, by bank card, by *shares* acquired without making any physical transfer. Stocks can in fact be sold before they are paid for, in microseconds that only a computer can calculate. The rich are the masters of time. And it's this domination of time, or the dematerialization of space by financial networks, that this book is all about, to denounce the deception and imposition of shameful servitude.

Capitalism is not only savage. It is vampiric as well as spectral. It haunts the world, drawing its grace from foodstuffs as much as from commercial services, speculating on advantages that no longer have any material counterpart[7]. It is bankrupting the ecology of the entire Earth. And those who enjoy these unconditional benefits no longer belong to any social class. Dematerialized masters have become

---

7. Speculation on hunger is heavily engaged by French banks according to the Oxfam association, which accuses BNP Paribas, Société Générale and BPCE via Natixis of providing their customers with tools enabling them to speculate on agricultural commodity prices to the tune of several billion euros. This jeopardizes the right to food (cf. *La Croix* newspaper, February 23, 2015) for hundreds of millions of people around the world. We couldn't think of a better way to bankrupt life itself.

unlocatable in terms of social class, often untraceable if the microseconds they enjoy are placed on the bangs of search engines (free for them, untaxed). They know how to use "pseudonyms" and multiple identifiers, without physical addresses. In this way, they slip through every loophole in the law to lead the world to its doom, destroying all social ties and all public assets, which they have become the predators of, while selling everywhere the holy, respectable image of debt. The ambition of this book is not only to denounce these actions, but also to highlight their criminal nature.

I / Globalization

Europe of Parasites

At no time in our history have we seen such an exorbitant increase in wealth. This is reflected in an astronomical amount of capital, which we won't go into here because it's so palpably obvious that it's unbearable. Yet the crisis is here, with its share of illusions whose tenacity should be denounced.

The crisis we're experiencing in Europe is actually a very profitable one. The destruction of work, its delocalization and increasing automation are irreversible. This mutation of forms of work allows us to make a profit which, instead of benefiting the community, is reinvested in financial accumulations, in speculation that organizes debt and takes advantage of the reorganization of forms of production, reducing the share of investment in the most traditional sectors of activity. We have moved on from Marx's historical materialism to the generalized dematerialization of capitalism. The word "sanitizing" is primarily a sanitary term, but it leads to the eradication of work itself, and the dismissal of those who appear to be parasites, useless to the functioning of a machine that, incidentally, no longer needs anyone. The vocabulary speaks for itself. There's no need for a particularly astute critic, or a pessimist with unionized language, to point it out. Nothing is invented when it comes to "de-fattening" companies, i.e. shedding the "fat", i.e. those who work. Cleanliness of 3D printers. Dirty sweaty workers. This "fat" is a word that in itself denotes the uselessness of the concept of work, which has become depreciatory. We no longer know what money, a significant part of which used to be used for the public good, is used for, if not perhaps the promotion of particular interests, the exacerbation of vain desires and endless pleasures, against everything that stands in the way of enjoyment, such as a labor code that is constantly denounced, or taxes, the payment of which is constantly circumvented. Facebook's bosses pay no more tax than a worker, as was recently revealed. The financial world, lined with marble, is turning away from work, seeking to capture all the planet's resources by increasing the interest rates on loans allocated to states every minute, directly deducted from our taxes to the point of undermining public interest budgets, be they those for health, education or even defense. The fact that interest rates on the borrowing market are falling is true for the banks, but not for the States under threat, denounced - here again - by the strange term of "bad pupils" singled out by European governance. Moralistic assessment is infecting the vocabulary of *politics*. Politicians are judged by specialists and graded like dunces at school. While the State is supposed to enjoy political autonomy, while taxation is supposed to guarantee the pooling of citizen creations, while it could be earmarked for human equality and the development of cultural values, the contributions extorted from us in the name of Europe or its debt actually serve to mop up interest rates whose existence is purely artificial and factitious. How can a world with profits in the hundreds of thousands of billions of dollars be in debt?

At the same time, this striking evolution in wealth corresponds to a world that now lives on poverty and unemployment, according to a law that is the inverse of the one laid down by Adam Smith[8]. We generally speak of "creators of wealth" to define those who get rich by resorting to the needs of secondary activities, the subcontracting necessary to achieve their ambition. Those with such an appetite would call on other hands to satisfy their greed, opening up various sectors of activity, creating a community of interests. But this logic seems to be reversed in the age of globalization. Instead of free enterprise and the selfishness of some enriching the regions that host it, it is poverty that now enriches the richest. The greed of those who seek personal profit hardly stimulates job creation, and the greed of those who open markets by speculating on wealth is no longer accompanied

---

8. As long ago as 1776, in *The Wealth of Nations,* Adam Smith spoke of an invisible hand, a kind of cunning that leads from the desire to enrich oneself to a collective benefit. Greed turns out to be the thread on which the public good and the creation of activities are built. This utilitarianism would be reason enough to justify the beneficial effects of capitalism.

by investment. Gone is the "invisible hand" that provided activities for all. Greed now lives in the short term, feeding on depression, disproportionate prices and meagre wages. Gains made through redundancies do not lead to investment. They merely multiply on the speculative level of stock market *shares*, volatile quotations with long-unverifiable claims. A company gains notoriety and value through layoffs and *depopulation*. It's no longer the hand that's invisible, but profit that becomes undetectable, speculative bubbles capable of fooling the most discerning.

As an extension of this capture of resources, all the wealth initially granted to States through taxation is now contested. Banks ceased to be popular, credit ceased to be mutual or agricultural, except to keep a slogan. So many names which still showed that their initial functions were put at the disposal of a common good. But the logic is obviously no longer that of communities, and money no longer depends on everyone's contribution. It is increasingly dependent on financial products, insurance premiums and even interest rates, which weigh down any common enterprise. The banking sector, or whatever collective word is used to describe it, is now governed by investors betting on the capital gains made on sometimes exorbitant, merciless loans, as can be seen in the catastrophe affecting the Greek people, whose shores and islands are being put up for sale and indecently privatized to pay off a debt that has become moral, pointed out as a *pupil*'s fault to be punished. Loans are granted to the public domain, with rating requirements whose pedagogy is above all profitable to the new masters of finance. The State, as the emanation of a people, is stripped of its power, having become incapable of negotiating rates. It is asked to show a little morality in its willingness to repay. It is required to ratify oppressions resulting from a savage domination that is no longer that of an identifiable class. The result is that the people are brought to heel in an apparent democracy subservient to the financial oligarchy. The state has become nothing more than a money-grabbing machine, an institution to which risk-free money is allocated, erasing the penalty that is usually incurred in other forms of shareholding involving the danger of losing what was invested.

The economic sphere's predation on state assets is based on financial arrangements over which politicians have lost all control. Any regulation, any taxation of banking transactions and products, seems doomed to failure, as is clearly the case for the "Tobin tax" which, quite recently, aimed to introduce greater clarity into the circulation of financial flows in Europe. Moreover, it is highly unlikely that Europe, as currently conceived, would have enabled us to cushion the crisis, a crisis that does not affect the financial market, a crisis distilled by skilful staging effects. A crisis distilled by skilful staging effects, as fearsome as any production of the imagination, as theatrical to legitimize the new powers born of European construction. And criticism of this insane mechanism itself becomes impossible. Any criticism is immediately dismissed as the rhetoric of the extremes, thrown back at the people as a moral and fascist fault. The perverse effect is that the destruction of jobs seeks to justify itself in the real world, unmasking and denouncing those who are not really responsible. So what crisis are we talking about? Is it a crisis engineered by fanciful companies? But fantasies die hard, and the destruction of reality has become irreversible. There is no crisis other than the one projected by an almost religious mirage, with limitless desires that seek their justification in reality: stalking, cuts and budget cuts blocking any European policy for greater solidarity and justice or with a social vocation, while profits have never soared so high!

Can the State still use the law against such deregulation, and can it uphold the legislator's political views? Instead of protecting us from a liberalism with no rules, no codes, no quid pro quo, boasting a freedom intolerant of all equality, Europe has become the cradle of apolitical thinking for which the public sphere is the virtuous substance, the lemon that must be squeezed to the last drop. In this purely managerial perspective, the power of the State, apparently mandated by the citizens according to prerogatives emanating from the people, constitutes a power to be brought down, or a democratic comedy to be staged through elections that no longer result in any action. The law is dead. An abject pretension to *undertake*, to suck in, to divert, to defiscalize, without any intervention other than that of a legal technocracy that exempts you from giving back to society the ill-gotten gains, exempt from the slightest tax while capturing the benefits of debt. The hydra of financialized capitalism lives off the backs of the States it vamps, while Europe offers it comfortable seats and a legality whose legitimacy is highly questionable. And there's no need to brandish the spectre of the Front National as a scarecrow when other thoughts and other criticisms are being tried out, which have nothing to do with nationalism. There's no question of criticizing Europe in favor of a return to policed nations, in order to give back the force of law to a state that dreams of authority, that seeks an exception for its violence. We can only assume that criticism of European directives will take on a different meaning from that of a return to the bâtonnier and the bars. Intellectuals cannot be forbidden to think against Europe on the pretext that discussion and opposition to the powers of the liberal economy form the nest of extremisms, these idols of the devil, these scarecrows brandished by capitalism. There is a spectre hovering over Europe today, and it is certainly not that of communism. A spectre made up of names that are still unlocatable, playing on relocation, untouchable by agreements we no longer want. For the time being, Europe only exists through the clever imagination of a few conjurers, who need to be made visible to the peoples who are its victims, and to whom they will have to answer historically for the vandalisms committed[9].

---

9. This sacralization of the economy was denounced by economist Bernard Maris in a number of his articles in *Charlie Hebdo* magazine. I point this out insofar as the events of January 2015 showed a mobilized people and a return to politics whose urgencies cannot suffer from a political recuperation of the movement.

Class Collapse

Taking into consideration the European debt issue is certainly a matter of specialization, of technical competence, but this will only produce figures, rarely a general logic. The priests of economics won't give us the slightest compass to read grids that make no sense in themselves. For example, statistics on working hours: according to the statistics, more people work in Germany than on the left bank of the Rhine. But the working hour is curiously more efficient in France than in Germany. It is more efficient, more laborious, precisely because working hours are shorter than elsewhere, so that personal investment is of higher quality. This conclusion is not drawn because it cannot be quantified. Nor can a teacher's working hours be compared or evaluated in terms of profitability. Not even that of a supermarket security guard, who produces nothing but whose work is undoubtedly hard. How can qualitative data be evaluated quantitatively? We simply superimpose figures which show that Germany, exempt from the 35-hour working week, has a longer half-yearly working time and that, on the other hand, efficiency will be higher in France, for reasons which are not explained. As for higher productivity, this is due to cross-border commuters, poorly-paid immigrants and more conciliatory rights for companies. The fact that excessively long working hours have an impact on efficiency and quality is an argument in favor of the 35-hour working week that is rarely considered when a company relocates to an area where there are no labor laws and no standards, with an obvious drop in product reliability. A squabble over figures, a measure is not an idea, far from it. But change, as Kant knew, lies in ideas, or, as he put it, in a "reform of understanding"[10]. Economics is content with statistics to bless what has already been achieved, a state of affairs that is compared with other facts elsewhere, in Germany, the UK, etc., in order to trumpet what works in the models taken as examples in the name of success, even when this success lives on in the bankruptcy of politics. There is a sacralization of efficiency, even that of a guillotine to be cited for the perfection of its mechanism. Democracy, then, is nothing more than theater, a theatrical effect to legitimize the interests of a barbaric capitalism, necessarily alien to political interests. All the figures put forward, all the so-called scientific and supposedly serious analyses respond to such an ideology without taking into account the place, the wealth of a locality, its physical and human geography. But this way of not thinking, this absence of thinking, can never silence the philosophical approach, precisely that of "political philosophy", which, as Aristotle would say, is bound to a place like no other. What works "here" cannot be a model for what might work "there". This is a strong and inescapable rule that no statistic can incorporate, and which explains the acquisition by foreign companies of national assets subject to infamous restructuring that cannot be reconciled with the quality of the work.

Understanding an era undoubtedly presupposes a reading that is out of step with the dominant discourse, but

---

10. This is the subject of Immanuel Kant's little opuscule, *Qu'est-ce que les Lumières* ? A fine translation by Françoise Proust and Jean-François Poirier, Paris, GF, 2006.

also a pamphleteering form to refute the majority opinion, the opinion that reasons on a global scale to found the pseudo-democratic beliefs that wield power, without any consideration for place, for locality. To *criticize means to* "adopt a higher point of view", but still a view immanent to the Earth's geography. Politicians seem to lack geographers, each aiming at what works abroad as if it were a simple importable recipe. Europe cannot mean homogenization of the means of production. We can't truly criticize without differentiating each touch of the system from a relocalized perspective. It's no longer just a case of Galileo no longer measuring movements from the Earth, but from an external position. Philosophy and history certainly offer an overhang, but with an attention to place that is not spoiled by the methods of enarches turned into clichés, with references that have become so common as to be taken as truth, committing us to imitate what works, to do as the others do, important the "Chinese miracle", the "German model" of work, the unbridled liberalism that is rampant in the United States as in Europe... And why not India, Bangladesh? Why not a France without a Labor Code? Isn't it this Code that's being singled out for criticism, even if it's Bayrou's moderate comments on a prime-time TV show - a man who no longer knows how to restore his image, how to get back on the scene? But others are beginning their comeback with recycled ideas on working hours, retirement at 67 in a country where everything is being done to leave it, to produce elsewhere, unconditionally, far from the law, in poor countries, not without dismantling activities and know-how, when people in their fifties are most often laid off because they're "too expensive". So how do we protect ourselves from the fantastic power of imitating what supposedly "works", the efficient models that thrive on deregulation and asymmetric trade?

If criticism of such a common trend is possible, it will only be possible by standing on the margins, on a boundary outside these pragmatic-looking discourses, which are so far removed from the reality of the people. And the concepts of "will" and "effort" to "stay the course" will not make a policy like that of a left that has just lost the very idea of politics. These are just empty words that fail to take the measure of the mutation of the world we live in. What we need to do is to explore a perspective that is free of fashionable interests. Take a look at history. To show that the crisis is consubstantial with a model of work, a change in modes of production, and therefore with a complex history that we need to unravel. A detour via Marx would certainly not be out of place to begin with, who understood that work, far from being a liberation, alienates us according to a hard service that subjects us to another, to a power that machine automation could have saved us from by lightening the task instead of seeing it monopolized by a rapacious minority. Marx was the only person in the 19th century to see a future in which working hours would be reduced and the means of production collectivized[11]. Marx's economic approach completely overhauled the categories of action, enabling

---

11. Karl Marx, *Principes d'une critique de l'économie politique (1857-58)*, Œuvres, Économie, Paris, Gallimard, la Pléiade, 1968, vol. II, p. 217 ff.

a different reading of the ideologies at play on the political stage. A scene that he compared to the comedy of opera buffa, to the dramatization of fetishes to make work sacred, to justify the action of a dominant class, a class that does not work but lives off the surplus value of those it places at its service by seizing the means of production privatized with the fall of the monarchy[12]. Together with Engels, he is the author of the incisive and pamphleteering *The Communist Manifesto*. Obviously, we don't think it's a good idea to reiterate its terms, which are no longer those of a conflict between the proletariat and the bourgeoisie, even if there are many struggles and fronts for which reading Marx would enable us to target the issues at stake. Undoubtedly, the word proletarian is no longer the most appropriate concept to describe the world of work or its disappearance. Humans are familiar with a division of labor that bears no resemblance to animal functions, to the great classes that can only be distinguished in an anthill or a beehive divided by instinctive traits. There's nothing like this in the human world, which is susceptible to history. The *subjects* and actors of politics have thus changed considerably, as we shall try to show with a brief reference to Foucault.

By renewing the categories for approaching work in a world that is no longer Marx's, the Marxist recourse to a

---

12. The idea of the fetish is analyzed by Marx in ways that would help us understand today how the image of Bernard Tapie, a level-headed sportsman, could be elevated by the symbolism of success, even to the point of acquiring a soccer club or a newspaper to endorse the symbolism of a brand. This fetishism of capitalism has already been exposed by Marx, for his own time, in Book 1 of *Capital*.

manifesto, this critical desire for a *manifesto,* is perfectly suited to the time of "crisis" that has hit us. A crisis that is now reaching its *critical* point. We're at a crucial moment, when *debt* is everywhere in the news, and a policy of debt is the only possible destiny for the State. But what kind of State are we talking about? Is it compatible with the art of governing, or is it perhaps more a desire to enslave, bypassing all true legality, when the purpose of proposing laws is to make enslavement possible, to favor those who dominate us? For all these reasons, it seems to us that there is no longer any such thing as *politics,* as the state scene has perhaps degenerated into a form of management that is not only comical but also sickly and self-denying, feeding the most shameless pretensions of what we now call *governance.*

Quitting

How can such a resignation be understood? How did such a story begin? We might consider that power can indeed escape those who are its purported subjects; it escapes through incapacity or negligence, so that the *governance* that names this impotence - purely technical, accounting governance - constitutes its *Regency*. Regency is generally a usurpation whose sole interest is to last through the retreat of law, through a purely technical and petty management of the law, temporary but lasting, a temporary that has become definitive. Arrangements that are given as temporary, but whose passage extends to all, thus reign. The exception becomes the rule. The examples of a Regency speak for themselves. But to understand the technocratic Regency of "governance", the buzzword for the retreat of politics in the face of Brussels' demands, we need to start at the beginning. And perhaps with the French Revolution, which indirectly kick-started this world.

In more ways than one, the French Revolution was a detour from its rightful course. It was not, of course, the exasperation of a few criminals storming the walls of the Bastille. Such a riot would have been quickly suppressed. Nor can we believe that today's "rioters", as is fashionable at every demonstration, can make history on the basis of a whim that has no claim to regularity. We'll need to say a few words to understand not only what we've inherited from the French Revolution, but also what has changed since then in the means of production and in the order of the *subjects who seized* them. More than "breakers", they are the "subjects" or "actors" of an opposition that has become classic - too classic, no doubt - that of proletarians in struggle with the bourgeoisie. There are undeniably subjects in conflict, and they belong to classes that can be defined according to a particular mode of production. Proletarians are neither serfs nor farmers. What we call man, in the modern era, is about to undergo a strange transformation, molding itself around other forms of activity that will transform it and draw it into contention with those who exploit it.

Perhaps it's hard to say what we are today, living out of place, caught up in listings and telephone servers that satellites can index. We're probably no longer proletarians, either at the factory or in the coal mine. At the time of the Revolution, there were no more proletarians. There was only the land, so to speak. And the peasantry was not yet the working class. It was tied to a place, a fiefdom. It was part of a particular way of producing in relation to the great landowners, the nobles, who had been losing the enormous capital they had built up through agriculture since the early eighteenth century. To understand us a little better today, let's go back for two minutes to those peasants who worked in the fields, still under the name of serfdom. Let's also remember those nobles who were not bourgeois, and who came under a different form of mastery than that of business creation. What happened before 1789 for a demonstration by a few individuals to degenerate into a considerable upheaval and impose itself on everyone as an event? Are we in a comparable climate in 2016? An attack is not enough to bring about change. We need to understand this kind of event in its insurrectionary mechanics in order to grasp the conditions of a historical mutation, the amplification of a revolt into a revolution. I'll do this very briefly, following an approach that Engels and Marx had at least foreseen in their 1845 work *The Holy Family*, an analysis in which the idea of the collapse of traditional classes founded on the power of families and the bonds of marriage dominates[13]. Today, it is no longer families, but brands, logos, the spirit of a subsidiary that can enjoy prestige. The family has been supplanted by the company. We are the children of subsidiaries, of filiations that are difficult to grasp, and which make us more abstract *executives* than technicians or engineers.

------

13. Karl Marx, *The Holy Family*, Paris, Éditions sociales, 1st ed., 1969.

But let's get back to the "holy family", which takes its name from a land, which comes from a place, with noble particles to signify a place (*de, du...*).

Revolt and Revolution

The French Revolution saw the emergence of new "subjects", who were not really part of a family line recognizable by genealogy, even if initially, in order to ennoble themselves, they sought to achieve a prestigious marriage, to anchor themselves in a place. There was no other way to become a master: earn a particle and benefit from the renown of nobility, let yourself be blessed by the choice of a wife. Immediately after the French Revolution, it was no longer marriage that provided a means of displaying social success through the purchase of a name and a dowry, even if the Restoration was to revive such a fantasy; however, it continued in literary accounts, as exemplified by the works of Dumas, before ending up in folklore today when the marriage of a princess is covered by the media. I wouldn't want to dwell too much on this ultimately inglorious, falsely moving episode, except to say that the emergence of a new social class, its soul, the spirit of a company, can only be achieved by wearing the mask of former prestige, by disguising oneself in the garb of those who apparently still wield power. A social costume that lasts for a very long time in the popular imagination, in a way that has become unconscious and fascinating. And in this collective imagination, the clergy was not to be outdone when it came to blessing unions. It's as if, in order to emerge and survive, the bourgeoisie first had to ennoble itself. In reality, what such a mask shows is that there was an invisible mutation, a change in power relations through a transfer of wealth throughout the 18th century. Land is apparently still a source of renown, the prestige of a name, but it is no longer what capitalizes, attracting those who are greedy for wealth[14].

The Age of Enlightenment, which made it possible for philosophers to criticize power and gave "intellectuals" an exceptional place, was a century turned towards innovation and technology, as evidenced by the *Encyclopédie*, which was intended to enable everyone to integrate the knowledge and codes of conduct of a society that had become modern. I won't go into detail about this mutation of knowledge, which was terrible for the monarchy, which didn't fully grasp what was at stake[15]. I will focus on another blindness,

---

14. At the beginning of the introduction ("La crise de l'Ancien Régime") to his book *La Révolution française* (Paris, "Terrains", Éditions sociales, 1982, *loc. cit.*, pp. 51-52), Albert Soboul writes: "Society remained aristocratic in essence, founded on the privilege of birth and landed wealth. But this traditional structure was undermined by the evolution of the economy, which increased the importance of movable wealth and the power of the bourgeoisie. At the same time, advances in positive knowledge and the conquering momentum of Enlightenment philosophy were undermining the ideological foundations of the established order. At the end of the eighteenth century, France was still essentially rural and artisanal, but the traditional economy was being transformed by the boom in commerce and the emergence of large-scale industry. The progress of capitalism and the demand for economic freedom were undoubtedly strongly resisted by social groups attached to the tradi-tional economic order, but they were no less necessary in the eyes of the bourgeoisie, whose philosophers and economists had developed a doctrine in line with its social and political interests. The nobility may well have retained the top rank in the official hierarchy, but its economic power and social role were in decline."

15. Hegel makes this diagnosis in his *Phenomenology of Spirit*.

the blindness that is the cause of political reversals, some of whose effects we can now also fear in the management of what we call "globalization". In fact, globalization is not so new. England ruled the world very early on, preparing the Commonwealth of the future with the influence of its fleet, at a time when France was still retreating to land ownership and the peasantry. In France, this retreat to the land was led by the nobility, who remained in their fiefdoms and châteaux, and saw no point in changing the forms of their production. Blindly, they delegated and abandoned these new production methods to a social category that was not clearly defined, and from which they succeeded in absorbing, through marriage, those individuals who had succeeded in making a profit from their "factories", their trading businesses - so many transactions that the nobility did not want. The latter obsessively linked the prestige of the name to land ownership, in a fundamentally feudal attitude. It is caught up in the roots, in the planted tree, in genealogy as the sole source of prestige. The exacerbated consumerism of the ruling classes, their taste for exotic products and market novelties, will undoubtedly contradict this withdrawal to the land and accelerate the ruin of the feudal edifice. But with this dual movement of seduction for luxury and retreat into the bosom of the family, economic regency was on the march.

Indeed, long before the French Revolution, there had been a growth in the consumption of manufactured goods, the benefits of which Colbert had tried to direct towards rationalizing production to free himself from Holland as an import agent, as well as from England. A raft of measures was implemented by Colbert, calling on the philosopher Leibniz to stabilize the anarchic development of wealth, but without succeeding in convincing a nobility that did not want to get its hands dirty by exploiting the assets beneath the earth[16]. The nobility, its particle, ignores the underground. They know only the surface, the most visible crust. In addition to this distaste for the underground, the nobility was hardly inclined to indulge in the creations of mechanics. It was this new manna that the bourgeoisie, still in its infancy, was to work and extract, making increasingly heavy industry possible, culminating in the advent - albeit very slow - of metallurgy, which would only become effective at the turn of the 19th century, as shown by the great urban architectures of the time, and the construction of ironworks that would make industrial society glorious.

This is the first form of relocation, from the land, the fiefdom, to underground riches that have to be painstakingly extracted through the creation of mines. It's a hellish task, a depreciation that contrasts with the joys of pastoral and religious life. This exclusion from emerging wealth, this abandonment by the nobility of the field of underground and mercantile activities, inevitably gave rise to a new social class, a new society. Those who work underground, or on the

---

16. On Colbert's relationship with Leibniz, see "Jean Baptiste Colbert, bâtisseur de la nation ou la politique du grand dessein" in [Collectif], *L'Europe, vecteur d'une reprise de l'économie mondiale*, Institut Schiller, 1992. Text out of print, available on the Web: http://www.solidariteetprogres.org/documents-de-fond-7/histoire/jean-baptiste-colbert.html

sea, like beasts of burden, and those, increasingly wealthy, who exploit or dominate them. Increasingly wealthy people who, instead of opposing the Ancien Régime, would first come to the aid of the nobility. The ruined nobility redeemed itself by offering the prestige of its name to the wealthier. They also wore this mask, ready to welcome the wolf or the black sheep into the fold. For the others, it will be a fall into the peasantry of the hobgoblins[17]. By the eve of the French Revolution, the wealth-generating activities of the nobility, exhausted and jaded in their libertinism, had completely disappeared. The nobility was deserted of all profits, and capital investment was finally channeled into other ongoing activities. Such processes are not simply a thing of the past. The contemporary economy is still inscribed in this logic, from which we perceive only the most superficial effects, certain events that must be read in a more subterranean light. In this respect, the Bastille Day event teaches us that it is nothing compared to the economic mutations of the eighteenth century. Such a symbol is merely the political manifestation of this profound, infrastructural mutation. A change without which the prisoners in question would quickly have returned to their dungeons.

Behind the street, there was another mask, family facades and the unleashing of all the economic interests resulting from a first "delocalization", from agrarian wealth to manufactured goods. It was these factories that Rousseau, tired

---

17. Michel Figeac's *Les noblesses en France du xvie au milieu du xixe siècle*, Paris, Armand Colin, 2013, is a good source of information.

of political struggles and ageing badly, denounced as sad figures of a new world, interrupting *Les Rêveries*, whose landscape was marred by industry. But underneath this still noble, pastoral perception, we sense a transfer of capital spurring the birth of a conflict that Rousseau knew was inevitable when he set about writing the *Social Contract*. A book banned in France, it circulated under the cloak and made Rousseau the enemy to be destroyed. In a way, the idea of a new society was at stake, underpinned by a quarrel whose protagonists would give rise to "subjects" - no longer the *serfs* in conflict with the *nobles*, but soon the *workers* in struggle with the *bourgeoisie* - even if Rousseau obviously didn't yet know what these subjects were to designate the new people he felt were growing up against the old world, any more than Hegel perhaps, who was still thinking in terms of *masters* and *servants*. It was Marx who would later reveal the subjects of history to come, under the name of the *proletariat* in conflict with the *bourgeoisie*.

Relocation of Heavy Industry

We can therefore understand that new subjects, new actors, are emerging on the world stage, with different interests: some are turning towards emerging activities, with maximum efficiency and profitability, while others, the workers, will be keen to use machine tools to lighten the conditions of exploitation. We're undoubtedly in another phase of renewal, but the logic behind these changes is not unrelated to the Revolution. In any case, we can see that the bourgeoisie very quickly focused on its own profit and detached itself from the tool. Its hobbyhorse is surplus value, not labor. It is interested in the tool, the means of production, not for the beauty of the machine, nor for the services it renders to human dignity, but quite simply for the savings it makes possible when the proletarian sees it as a glorious instrument, a liberating creation and workforce. We're all too familiar with this different approach to self-interest to repeat it here. I'd rather focus on a more profound delocalization, which explains the globalization that now characterizes our existence. And to measure the scale of this mutation, I'll have to follow the modes of production that run through recent history. In fact, the driving force of this history begins with the relocation of capital, which is not interested in things, but is constantly moving elsewhere, from the products of the earth to the more sophisticated consumer goods produced by technology. This new need led first to the creation of heavy industry, which exploited raw materials. This was the source of new wealth, no doubt at the same time as the circulation of exotic products (cotton, cocoa, tea, coffee). It's about a relationship with matter, a materialism that places the proletarian at the center of such a system of objects, with the trades employing a prolific workforce. But things can't be reduced to such a fixed relationship, to a caricatured opposition of "bourgeois" and "proletarian". Distinctions are finer, more complex. A new mutation is underway, one that sees the emergence of new subjects: the engineer, the technician, abandoning the natural realm of *things* in favor of *objects*. There are no objects without manufacture, only things of the earth. The world became a world of objects with the birth of industry. And objects are interesting not as substances, but as vectors of exchange.

The capitalization of wealth through the exploitation of what had become heavy industry was not an end in itself, and the bourgeoisie itself diversified its activities to meet more profitable requirements. By the middle of the 19th century, this diversification led to new forms of industry: the *processing industry*. This more technological mode of objectification competed with heavy industry, which still focused on substances and materials. Manufacturing and assembly plants were born, bringing traditional forms of exploitation to their knees, as in the case of mining resources. Zola's novel *Germinal makes* literary use of this transformation. The riches of the soil no longer germinate, but are imported from elsewhere. Trade dissolves the reign of things. It is this unfair import that competes with all local farms, de-substantiating them. They will, moreover, have to adjust their wages to lower prices as a result of the saturation of products obtained abroad at lower cost. It's the profit margin that interests the bourgeoisie, not the product of labor. As a result, working conditions changed, in the face of competition from higher profit margins through imports. The codification of such a competitive space, and the rules of such a game, will be won through long-term struggles. The proletariat was to become unionized, giving rise to the Labor Code so decried today by Medef and, more recently, by the political class itself, whose motto was freedom and equality. The gradual relocation of heavy industry, driven by the lure of profit, has certainly given rise to unfair competition, impoverishing the poor with a poverty that has become unbearable. New revolts were in the air. And they were to find a national echo through the birth of social ideas, notably those of Proudhon, ideas that were to modify events and the balance of power between subject and object in a conflict whose outbursts capitalism managed to contain.

The crisis brought about by this rampant relocation of heavy industry and the materials it increasingly imports, is easily and quickly absorbed by the creation of new wealth, by the transformation of raw materials from elsewhere, whose exploitation has been entrusted to other sectors of the geography. The bourgeoisie relocates relocation in droves, with new job profiles linked to the transformation of objects. Elaborate technical activities are born, calling on technology and technicians who are no longer quite comparable to proletarians in terms of lifestyle, standard of living and demands. The transformation of things into objects presupposes practices that involve instruction, the democratization of knowledge and technical acquisition. It's a new actor, a new *subject* in capitalist society, cushioning, so to speak, the relationship between employers and workers. Such a transformation will have required considerable training efforts. It needed schools. It is not a concession to the proletariat to exempt its children from the heavy work of the mine. It was absolutely not out of fairness, but to meet the new needs of the transformation industry, a complex transformation that could only be achieved through theoretical skills acquired in schools, which had rapidly become secular and in touch with the realities of society, whose needs were far removed from religious training. A new form of knowledge was born, with objectivity and profitability recognized by the production of objects. This explains why the crisis caused by the import of raw materials is quickly cushioned by the labor that transforms them, by the consumables of technology and by the education that teaches new technologies.

The relocation of heavy industry was acceptable until the last quarter of the 20th century, when the last mines, the last symbols of workers' and metallurgical power, were gradually closed (Florange, among many other plant closures, was the last hiccup). But at the same time, the transformation that is so profitable is itself in the process of being abandoned, relocated, when not dematerialized by 3D printers. And there's no other way to explain the discredit that is damaging the image of the teacher, who is becoming a burden today, to the point of making it conceivable to abandon school, close classrooms and privatize studies, which have become a luxury or a leisure activity. Teachers no longer have engineers to train. Putting teachers to work has no other meaning than to point up their uselessness in a system that no longer needs to transform matter, nor needs technicians, and consequently, instructors... If the transformation industry has thus succeeded in its entry into history, with its cohorts of baccalaureate holders and engineers, who constitute the glory of the 20th century, this glory is all relative and will see its power progressively eroded by new relocations. Integral dematerialization, the advent of immaterials and virtual forms, render all dialectical materialism and communism based on the proletarian structure of labor obsolete.

The specialized worker, the engineer and the technician are replaced by the consultant, the financial advisor or the *trader*, who are far from being researchers.

The Death of the Processing Industry

After the relocation of agrarian modes of production to the subsoil, what was needed was a more unbridled relocation, with new basins of attraction under the pretext of progress, but whose sole driving force will be greed. As a result, new forms of enslavement are emerging that are no longer solely linked to the import of raw materials. In part, this involves colonization and, following its ultimate decline, the implementation of immigration to provide the most difficult services. Colonization and immigration are part of the same form of exploitation. Either the subjugation of peoples outside their borders, or the integration of repatriated servants for the vilest tasks, a workforce in emergency, on the run en masse, ready to serve a master who recognizes them only as a means of production, a part of a machine, a cog that can be degreased at will. Slavery first intensified as the bourgeoisie developed new needs and more sophisticated consumption patterns, at the same time as a slow decline in agriculture began in the eighteenth century. A complex mechanism, insensitive at first, but which encouraged the emergence of plantations and farms of all kinds in distant lands, producing cotton, sugarcane, manioc, coffee and rubber. It is only on this condition that we can understand why serfs in Europe freed themselves from the tutelage of the rich, becoming handlers and consumers. This was not made possible by the clemency of the ruling classes, but by the relocation of slavery, agricultural exploitation and labor power to a new slavery in a colonizing world. The colonialists were responsible for clearing the land. And the technological revolution that will soon relocate heavy industry will undoubtedly have comparable effects in terms of human exploitation to those caused by the colonial transfer of agriculture, which has become exotic. Raw materials, increasingly imported, require the hardest work to take place elsewhere, making us Europeans like the good Swiss, innocently banking on the beauty of our landscapes without feeling the slightest guilt, little aware that we are living off the backs of a slavery that has become universal. Capitalism, the surplus value on which those who dominate are fattened - and which Marx was the first to discover as a mechanism of exploitation - is inseparable from a logic of slavery, a logic that Hegel and then Marx would call *alienation*. Thus, the first philosopher to take the side of the slave against the master was Hegel, at a time when a revolt was taking place, a successful riot in Haiti, an uprising of slaves singing *La Marseillaise* overseas against French soldiers[18].

Taking advantage of this cheap labor, which cost only the stick and the whip, and profiting from the passivity of the oppressed, Western countries, in a way, were content to transform and recompose materials according to the processes of chemistry and nascent mechanics. In the background, the humanitarian idea of enlightening peoples,

---

18. Susan Buck-Morss, *Hegel et Haïti*, Paris, Éditions Lignes-Léo Scheer, 2006.

evangelizing them for the salvation of their souls, for their spiritual good. To the spiritual gift of the masters was added the idea of a debt owed by the enslaved. At the same time, a new model of education was born, a school that did not simply emerge from the good conscience of the bourgeoisie to educate the humble. It's a school of freedom in appearance, but above all a school of surplus value. Grafted onto the learning of new exploitation and transformation techniques, the dream of educating, the idea of progress, of liberation through the machine, all the utopias of positivism sometimes relayed by a certain Jules Verne, whose heroes are indeed "engineers" and "colonists". It's a world conquered, subjugated by knowledge that benefits above all the Gun Club, the wealthy arms dealers Verne describes with humor, who give in to progress during the rare periods of truce. But this utopia of progress, as everyone can see today, now turns into a nightmare, as modernity leads to nothing but *expense*, to an economy that Georges Bataille diagnosed at the time of Hiroshima, showing that the profit, the surplus-value of the capitalist system ends up paying for the means of death, by sinking into the power of planetary destruction[19]. It's a beautiful dream that's crumbling today, even if technology is capable of creating extraordinary living conditions. And this

---

19. According to Bataille, the sum of energy produced is always greater than the need, and this surplus value of production is aimed at pure expenditure, at the pleasure of enslaving and subjugating others through the means of this wealth. For Bataille, surplus value is the accursed part. The economy is subject to the principle of this expenditure, accumulating in order to destroy and cause suffering until the Earth is extinct, cf. *La Part maudite*, preceded by *La Notion de dépense*, Paris, Éditions de Minuit, 1967.

is happening in a Europe that is shrinking, an anemic Europe, a lawless spectre that is helping to promote its expansion through a final delocalization, that of the light enterprise, the processing industry to so-called emerging countries.

The Global Era

We've moved on to a new speed of communication, consumption and the dematerialized exploitation of resources by increasingly sophisticated digital machines... What "subject" corresponds to this advent, what "wild *cogito*" for this world where immaterials and virtual wealth reign? The French Revolution was not just the fall of the monarchy, but culminated in a frenzied individualism in which everyone aspired to become king. The king is dead, long live the new kings! With needs, palaces and luxuries that make ownership a concern and threaten the planet with asphyxiation. The system of inheritance is reconstituting empires within empires, domains and accumulations of wealth that constitute veritable cartels, partisan groups that reign over globalization. It's no longer simply heavy industry, which is primarily attached to the soil, that's relocating. The contemporary crisis is linked to the relocation of the processing industry itself, after having first favored immigration flows for cheap labor. The transplantation of manufacturing was initially carried out for the benefit of the so-called middle classes, whose sole activity was trade and the provision of services: an activity that has become essentially tertiary. Today, the world of work has abstracted its products even further, without any real production, contenting itself with distribution alone, or even with communication, advertising and marketing monopolized by the dominant financial classes born of absolute delocalization. Sovereignty is obviously no longer political. Political options take a back seat to the reign of values and exchange. It is utility that makes man, utilitarianism that defines him, and no longer language, *logos*, the activity of thought. The "public service" appears to be of little interest in a world such as this, which is aimed at the profit of a minority - 1% of the population holding more than half the world's wealth, while the other 99 are only there to pay off the debt[20]. In such circumstances, it doesn't matter what is being sold, as long as it fits in with the strategy of gilded communication. The modern subject is no more than a number on a telephone listing that reduces everyone to a potential consumer, a communicable commodity with auto-mated, robotic mass telephone calls that call us for products whose only interest is that of not corresponding to any need. And to sell these useless products, we invoke official surveys, ministries and economy plans that give us an idea of the decrepitude of the State. The successive policies of the 21st century are invoked only as a palliative, to justify the cunning investigation of those who target us with the idea of selling renewable energy or saving energy through tax exemption. As for the free Internet, it enables tax-free share trading. However, such a network does not come without the need to track down every individual, who becomes a data manna for selling the most insipid objects, or even the number of clicks

---

20. Report published by the *Oxfam* organization in January 2015.

or *likes* on a digital page. This kind of sales activity, which has become so volatile as to constitute social networks, a virtual city, has been taking shape since the end of the Second World War, which had triggered the need to transform elsewhere, to reject matter outside a society that had become pure. Taking advantage of this increasingly abstract movement, European companies sought to generate enormous capital gains by shifting their industries to cheaper labor, thus creating a new form of slavery with dramatic consequences. At the frontiers of the Western world, a new hell was born.

So we have to accuse, accuse the trait, even if the taste for accusation has gone out of fashion, not against the little pickpockets in front of the undoubtedly guilty luxury department stores, but just as much against the luxury stores themselves. We need to accuse in the manner of Zola in his day. We must accuse these *chic and fashionable department stores,* accusing them not only of encouraging the flight of know-how and jobs that have been destroyed on a massive scale, without a care in the world, but also of promoting the infamy of a logic that accompanies their now spectacular profits, a profit that thrives on "downsizing" without number, on the solicitation of foreign companies that are called in without even questioning the safety conditions or the age of the children working there. This idea of human "downsizing" does not come from our suspicious imagination. It has been the technical, clean, surgical name to justify unemployment in France. There was talk of *cleaning up* companies as if the workers and senior technicians were unhealthy, the name of a disease, fatness, a virus in a society that no longer tolerates unattractive weight figures. This was the time when Bernard Tapie became a star of success by relocating Adidas and many other companies. At the same time, he was invited to appear on *Gym Tonic* to sing the praises of sport. Downsizing is the obnoxious name that has become polite and technical as politics becomes governance, not to mention other journalistic terms that turn Greek demonstrators protesting about being cheated into "thugs". These names are repeated over and over again by all journalists, and once by the left-wing Minister of Education, Claude Allègre, who was proud of his quip that he had to "slim down the mammoth". Lose its weight, and in a way break up the civil service, which is no longer compatible with the new capitalism now protected by a regent state. Now, the wealthiest have their villas - such as the Corsican villa of an actor very close to an ex-president of the Republic - guarded without having to pay a private militia, as is necessary in developing countries. The militia is now provided by a simulacrum of a state, what's left of it in terms of pompous image and presence.

The result is a policy of communicators who set the example of deregulation and who will impose themselves on companies, which are effectively living on the brink of asphyxiation, stifling all creation for the sake of globalization. We must legitimately accuse such words, such evils. It's up to us, as citizens, to accuse, with all our might and strength, these great Houses, these great Brands that no longer have a mammoth to slim down, the great ones of this world who have lost their greatness by thinking only of destroying what is Great. They are the architects of what is ugly, making ugliness the only resource of life, without anyone condemning them for this devitalization. The delinquents we hunt down every day pale into insignificance compared to the supreme theft committed in the name of wealth, the rapacity of the creators of destruction[21], organizing at European level the transfer of capital to Switzerland or Luxembourg to avoid being taxed, while at the same time taxing Greece, which is obliged to buy back its public debt at abusive interest rates (when the statues on its monuments have been stolen by all European museums, which refuse to return these cultural assets, and when Germany refuses to pay Greece the 7 billion dollars in war reparations it owes under the Paris Agreements of January 14, 1946)[22]. It seems to us that the time has come to

---

21. This is an opportunity to quote Louis-Ferdinand Céline, who wrote these powerful and very true sentences in Le *Voyage*: "Certainly, we are in the habit of admiring immense bandits every day, whose opulence the whole world venerates with us, and whose existence is demonstrated as soon as we examine them closely as a long crime each day renewed, But these people enjoy glory, honors and power, their crimes are enshrined in law, while as far back as history goes - and you know I'm paid to know it - everything shows us that venial petty theft, This is for two reasons: firstly, because the perpetrator of such crimes is generally poor, and this state of affairs in itself implies a capital indignity; and secondly, because his act carries with it a kind of tacit reproach towards the community. Stealing from the poor becomes a mischievous individual reprisal, don't you see? Where would we go? This is why the repression of petty theft is practiced, note, in all climates, with extreme rigor, not only as a means of social defense, but also and above all as a stern recommendation to all unfortunates to remain in their place and in their caste, happily resigned to dying throughout the centuries and indefinitely of misery and hunger" (*Voyage au bout de la nuit*, Paris, Denoël et Steele, 1932, p. 84-85).
22. "The 226.9 billion euros lent by eurozone countries to Greece were not at zero interest. At the time of the first aid plan, they made a "margin" of 300 basis points (i.e., if they themselves borrowed at 1.5%, they lent to Greece at 4.5%). Lucrative, even abusive, so much so that these rates were subsequently revised downwards. Transparency, however, is not the order of the day. Only

criticize the categories of what passes for *Good* and what is shown to be *Evil*, the time to denounce this engeance with clean hands and a dirty heart, which hides behind morality, scandalizes the homeless, displays a compassed air in front of the poor, while creating slavery for all to see, robbing the weak, the weak of all miserable countries. We still have to admit that we can laugh at the dentures of the humble, between the teeth that, in so doing, rattle the caviar, splattering their remains, their waste, all that lives, all those who will be afraid of it without feeling the miserable stench that emanates from it. Don't we feel the taste of a corpse crushed under the weight of working conditions that increasingly claim to be deregulated, demanding labor without any conditions, without any codes?

---

the European Financial Stability Facility (EFSF) claims to lend at a rate of 1.5%, and certifies that this rate does not guarantee it any income, just enough to cover the loan it took out to lend to Greece, as well as its operating costs. For bilateral loans, rates vary from country to country. For France, Bercy prefers to give a global figure. Since 2010, over four years, loans to Greece have brought in 729 million euros, which has been entered as revenue in the State budget. This is more or less the amount budgeted for the French Ministry of Culture in 2015. However, this is a gross figure, which does not take into account the interest France had to pay for the loan it took out to lend to Greece. As for the ECB, since 2010 it has been buying Greek Treasury bonds, which also earn interest. It's hard to know exactly how much. From sources close to the ECB, it is estimated that these Greek treasury bonds have yielded over 2 billion euros a year in interest since 2010. A colossal amount. In 2010, 2011 and 2012, it was the central banks of the euro zone (Bundesbank, Banque de France, etc.) that collected this money (as the ECB buys Greek Treasury bonds through them, they are the ones who receive the interest on these securities). For three years, the Greek crisis has been lucrative for its European creditors. Cf. *Les Matins de France Culture*, broadcast on June 30, 2015, "Tout comprendre de la dette grecque en six étapes".

II / The Subjects of Globalization

New Subjectivities

Today's world is saturated with dream merchants who create nothing but nightmares, disease, epidemics and abjection. Liberalism is devoid of all spirituality. It has no end in sight, not even progress, which no longer interests it, retaining only the most self-serving, least innovative forms of technology. Once immediate profitability has been asserted, there is little future to offer, and it's astonishing that people can turn to religion for a little salvation. Plato must have argued with Protagoras that man's value cannot be reduced to utility and quantifiable production, nor to the possibility of working better or more. Man is a thinking being[23]. Without hope, without consideration for ideas, liberalism runs on empty, denouncing all meditation as religious, ideological or extremist ranting. It's up to us

---

23. Read Hannah Arendt's fine commentary on Plato in *La Condition de l'homme moderne*, Paris, coll. "Agora", Pocket, p. 211-213.

to thwart this machine, which claims to be moral even as it crushes living bodies, sold as carcasses of meat, bones, soon to be offal recycled with all the gloss of packaging or the musical glitz of a few supermarkets. Philosophy's critical sense cannot subscribe to the program of these gut-wrenchers, these horse-eaters who treat men like cattle, and who, in their slaughterhouses, inject polyphosphates into the carcasses to sell us the surplus water, the weight of this cheap liquid at the price of meat. Do we no longer have any dignity, no longer have the strength of the Haitian slaves who revolted and whom Hegel admired at the very beginning of the 19th century? Haven't masters, as Hegel shows, become even more useless, even worse than in those supposedly barbaric times? Today's speculation promises a more insidious, but also more rapid success, that of the nouveau riche, who are more oblivious than their ancestors, who didn't count on the chance of a quotation to celebrate their gods. And if slavery has been abolished, even supposing that colonialism was perhaps also motivated by good civilizing intentions, what are we to think today of the delocalization of work? And, consequently, of the downsizing that affects the humble, induced by the cheap production made possible by modern slavery? We seem to have been reduced to *Vivre et penser comme des porcs*[24] to borrow a title from Gilles Châtelet. In reality, no one is accusing the

---

24. *Vivre et penser comme des porcs* (Living and thinking like pigs) is the title of an essay by mathematician Gilles Châtelet, Paris, Éditions Exils, 1998, reissued in paperback, Paris, coll. "Folio actuel" (n° 73), Gallimard, 2000.

Debt Slavery

golden boys who, far worse than pigs, behave like wolves[25]. The upstarts who form the "ideal of the self" assumed by every shareholder, the model of the entrepreneurial spirit to sell everywhere their guilty conscience, their undue tax exemption, their titles of nobility, their actions de grace, their smiles whitened by artificial paradises we no longer want, with as no other consequence the deterioration of the world's resources of intelligence, energy and beauty. And we must speak of a new slavery when workers are buried under the walls of their Bangladeshi factory, without rights, barely paid by the luxury brands and major clothing chains, who decline all responsibility, blaming the production standards of countries that have precisely been selected for their lack of standards, for the low cost of their so liberal production.

The question then arises as to what we Europeans have become today, which subjects, which actors we idealize by admiring the model of success that our leaders show us as being that of work, when those who don't work simply rake in the money from speculation. Do we have to get up very early to benefit from a machine that runs so far away, abroad, under the control of infamous men? If the subjects of the agrarian economy were the *serfs* and the *nobles*, if those of the industrial economy were the *proletarians* and the *bourgeois*, what is our name now, we Europeans of today? Slave, shareholder, communicator? And is the corresponding

---

25. See Jordan Belfort's book *Le Loup de Wall Street* (The Wolf of Wall Street), published by Max Milo in 2009, and the film Martin Scorcese made from it in 2013, starring a dazzling Leonardo DiCaprio.

pathology that of the stress of losing, the burn-out of those who check exchange rates every morning? But that would still be too mild, too convenient to describe a much darker reality. We need to start by showing that there are obviously no longer any proletarians. Since the advent of globalization, the "subject" of action is no longer the worker. His or her labor power is no longer worth anything, when each individual is no more than a connection identifier, an IP address, now the product of collection by computer robots, search engines, e-mail histories and geolocalized telephone payments.

To the delocalization of production methods is added the automation of a new localization, the geolocalization of all those who enter the large network, who are canvassed to respond to paid messages, to highly-taxed numbers, to boxes with no human addressee, to voice messaging. So, the actors who govern us are the invisible ones who own the automatons that manage and collect our consumption habits. Consumers, modes of consumption rather than modes of production define the new contemporary subjectivity. The opposition is no longer that of bourgeoisie and proletariat. Other actors manipulate the electronic programs and networked machines that govern global exchanges from one sector of the planet to another. Faced with such power, the only resistance, the only subjective resource, becomes the ability to make oneself invisible, a quest for invisibility. But it's really a question of a double inconsistency, a double invisibility. There are those, the most affluent, who usurp anonymous programs, who hide behind robots that calculate the flow of shares on the stock market in nanoseconds, and who are neither traceable nor taxable. And then there are those, the most destitute, who refuse to be reduced to a number, a name on a list, on an advertising server, and try to leave the network. Mozilla's crusade against Google is no different, offering us the chance to rediscover an insurvised life, to conquer the rather illusory tools of a so-called *private* mode of connection. Computer invisibility is relative. It applies to those who dominate and organize the network. But it is seriously compromised for the careless users we have become. The subject of the contemporary world is unable to retreat into the space of intimacy, as everyone is exposed to absolute transparency, even behind the doors of his or her bedroom, a victim of *capitalist sorcery*[26]. Capitalism knows no intimacy. Although it criticized communism for suppressing property, it can only offer us a meagre private life when our bodies and souls no longer belong to us and have become the subjects of total surveillance[27], as if subjected to drones or ghosts that pass through walls, observe our meagre resources and steal their circulation. It is notable that it is the banks that are now offering private individuals video surveillance systems and agents to intervene in the private space of the home. Control of your accounts, health insurance and living space in a single package. This speaks volumes about the shifts in power in modern times.

---

26. *La sorcellerie capitaliste,* by Philippe Pignarre and Isabelle Stengers, published by La Découverte in 2005.

27. Michel Foucault was the first to show how our society is moving towards total surveillance in *Surveiller et punir,* Gallimard, 1975, as was Deleuze in a short text entitled "Post-scriptum sur les sociétés de contrôle" in *Pourparlers,* Paris, Éditions de Minuit, 1990, pp. 240-247.

State Bankruptcy

The writer William Boyd, in a novel describing a hunted character, shows quite clearly that the identification of the suspect follows hitherto unknown procedures. These coordinates speak volumes about the contemporary treatment of subjectivity. Subjectivity can only survive in places where it becomes invisible, where it disappears, avoiding all the boundaries and thresholds that make it perceptible. Indeed, to avoid appearing in society's computer scan, we have to abandon our cell phones and bank cards, wandering in the marginal space of a suburb that is the banished suburb of the Network, in the image of *Matrix*, which also proposes a parallel life. In truth, it's impossible. The only resistance to power would be to become undetectable, to leave no trace, thus entering the clandestinity of the *disappeared* who haunt the great capitals[28]. And it's obviously no longer a question of a "social class", but rather of an erratic subject, a subject who wanders between classes to cross the grids of information technology, to escape the Spirits who lie in wait at every step. This invisibility is sometimes the result of luxury, sometimes of escape: Either major financial delinquents have the means to erase their tracks, to launder their identities in order to escape the Web's historical records; or petty criminals endeavor to bypass the means of communication, or to use networks that can't be traced, if at all; or they use their technical know-how and computer tools to create a viral process

---

28. William Boyd, *Orages ordinaires* (Ordinary Storms), Paris, Éditions du Seuil, 2011.

that will *hack into* the global network and discover how to surf like a pirate... *Pirate* means the *worst*. He who enters the limit (from the Greek *peira, peirátēs*). It's an *ex-perience* (periplus, periphery, are indeed compound words from the same root). A moment of danger for the subject who disappears, who is struck off the list but at the same time takes the risk of losing himself, as Neo would do in The *Matrix*. Such a subject could be *Anonymous,* as we saw when they targeted the addresses of jihadists on Twitter, siding with *Charlie...* *It's* a strange subject, in fact, which transits from one side to the other according to interests that are not clear-cut, which are sometimes related to piracy and sometimes to the most fruitful exchanges, blurring the boundary between delinquency and finance. It's easy to see that the subject of this space, whose standards are so heterogeneous and volatile, oscillates between piracy, which resists all law, and mafia networks, which make themselves accomplices to data transparency, sometimes businessmen, sometimes informers, sometimes free-riders... Outside the law, playing with it when necessary, this subject doesn't enter the network of visibility and assumes multiple identities. This is not the case for the average citizen. They remain passive in this new form of power, which ranges from *hacker* to *trader*. He or she is unaware of this computerized routing, reduced to a simple unconscious surfer, a user, an advertising target whose IP will be recorded by a database, an address book to be exploited like a docile material.

In any case, it's hard for the user to remain, as Heidegger thought, in the reign of the "we", to take on the role of

"Mr. Everyman" when the planetary domination of information exploits our every desire, our every inclination, under the vigilance of robots that watch over us, turning at night, while we sleep, to exploit our *cookies*, our footsteps on the web of the Net. A watch that occurs according to the "standby mode" of intentionless machines, monitoring our movements in the name of total security, a security that is video-monitored, the entire planet having been transformed into mappemondes and maps that are easy to cross-reference, allowing a space dominated by *traceability* to emerge. The subject of a globalized society is no longer reducible to a class, but to populations affected by barcodes, traces that form the signs of it, computer signals, bank digitization signals, telephone signals In each of these networks, he is assigned an identifier to mark his passage into the population of numbers into which he will merge for a short while, but passes elsewhere very quickly. He is evaluated by the speed of this passage: a whole statistic of groups, spheres of influence, communication power. Its power, its glory, will be a function of its capacity to resonate in broadcasting systems, to cross the maximum number of populations.

Power is no longer measured by what is built, but by *kilolinks*, by what moves at the speed of light, according to the computerized dimension of finance, bank prices and quotations. Prices measured by robots according to a temporality that is no longer human, made possible by the machine. Greece, for example, is obliged to make massive calls for funds. The purpose of these calls is to cover a real debt. But we don't know how much of the incentive has been created by the banks themselves, who are capable of dangling their indecent offers in advance, as groups like Goldman Sachs seem to be accused of doing. The most sordid forms of debt organization can be imagined by way of hypothesis. Real debt is undoubtedly superimposed on virtual debt, which is not in part unrelated to the Greek situation, and which can be managed at computer speed. Greek debt may well be bought and *dematerialized* before the finger is pointed, then sold like a commodity to those who think they can promise more profits and resell it for even more, until the debt becomes unbearable and therefore unpayable[29]. Profit presupposes no real investment. It comes from the promise made to the borrower by a *trader* who never shows his hand. The first buyers, those who speculate upstream, will have made a quick profit by selling their promise to an impossible-to-clear population of small lenders and pensioners, whose account numbers remain virtually untraceable, covered by banking secrecy. At first, the risk was low. But the debt is resold, with each intermediary paying ever-increasing interest in a timeframe so short that it is no longer palpable, a timeframe that falls within the realm of "nanotechnology", inferior to the possibility of tracing it. Debt has thus been artificially created. It is weighed down by those who are quickest to resell it, the most anonymous. It swells in circulation until it becomes unpayable. This is what we call a speculative bubble, a bubble that inflates, and will continue to inflate as

---

29. On this subject, see Pierre-Noël Giraud, *Le Commerce des promesses. Petit traité sur la finance moderne,* Paris, Éditions du Seuil, 2001.

it passes through buyers who will make a profit each time, without paying a cent.

This increase in debt doesn't really exist; it has been artificially created by the mere *promise of* a profitable rate, and the debt is passed on to the next borrower, helping himself in the process. The fact that the rate is falling, as announced, to less than 1%, is not even a favour to France, whose acquisition of "bons du Trésor" at a historically low rate conceals the fact that this loan is being used to repay a large part of the debt already contracted. In other words, it's a 1% increase on the interest already contracted, a low percentage that appears to be conceded only to repay a sum already heavily penalized by previous rates. So it's more a question of additional interest, loop interest, skimmed off a given sum of money to be immediately returned to the creditors, with an additional capital gain captured on old interest relating to the overall debt, which is totally astronomical... And this process of debt circulation would probably not exist without the computer arsenal that accelerates the speed of transactions in a time that is no longer a matter of human exchanges, and therefore impossible to tax. It resembles an ever-expanding snowball, rolling over itself and its debtors. But this sphere can only be filled by air, by wind, to the point of bursting speculative illusions in a generalized crash. And the Greeks had nothing to do with it, except to have launched the initial call for a loan to cover a real deficit, deemed immoral, linked to the supposed lightness of a southern population lacking the Germanic sense of work. The moral of this story is as trivial as that of *La Cigale et la Fourmi*. No doubt many banks will have rushed to grant easy loans, offering more than they needed in a clever, impossible-to-establish way. As the SwissLeaks revelations show, some Swiss banks were themselves ready to organize capital flight to France and elsewhere, thereby arranging the entire European tax-free protocol. We can imagine that it was no different when it came to plugging artificial debt in countries whose governments were on the verge of bankruptcy.

Digital Subjectivity

Here we are in a new form of subjectivation, between trader, *hacker, anonymous, Charlie There were, of* course, preconditions to this rise of virtual subjectivity. Pierre Macherey attempts to approach this new form of subjectivation in a recent book that doesn't really deal with computer processes, and is therefore very different from our own point of view. It does, however, show how numerous norms are being put in place that no longer bear the outline of a class. The subject passes through the interweaving of norms specific to different populations. There are conflicting sets of norms, bundles of norms that are capable of welding together or destroying each other, not without devaluing long-acquired rights, or even creating new ones. These unstable games lead to a *subject of standards*[30]. Macherey, without yet taking on board the electronic dimension of a society dominated by the watchful eye of robots and the cross-referencing of personal data and IPs that characterize

---

30. Pierre Macherey, *Le sujet des normes*, Paris, Éditions Amsterdam, 2014.

us, nevertheless captures the right tone with regard to our power to direct ourselves in such a normative space. It's an orientation that involves means of pinpointing and tracking, and, at the same time, new forms of resistance on our part in the face of a "power" that is no longer solely that of the bourgeoisie, and which is far from being reduced to the form of the state. Of course, it would never occur to us to embark on an apology for the state, which is always, in the last instance, a policeman in search of an exception to the law. But it is possible to imagine a form of State that is like a collective person, defending the interests of all and the singularity of each individual, while respecting differences. The state as a screen for dominating classes, forcibly oppressing the weakest, is clearly a Leviathan that no philosophy worthy of the name could wish for. We have experienced too many terrors to appeal to the State or submit to "voluntary servitude". We have shared the cries of alarm of our time, from Kafka to Huxley to Orwell and other forms of resistance to power. It would be far better to think of the future state as a "counter-power" rather than as a power. A political claim that is the organized gathering of forces of insubordination, as might have been the case in Greece, by a people asserting its sovereignty in the face of the economic directives that are suffocating it. As things stand, we have to recognize that the retreat of politics is not at all the advent of communism, nor of a classless society. Or at any rate, if it is classless, as we shall see, it will not be without savagery. The state, the target of classical communism, which dreamed of seeing it disappear, is indeed disappearing, and not by the will of a society that would have fought frankly, with dignity, against the repression of those who exploit and dominate it.

The State has evaporated through its inability to set the rules of the democratic game. Law has been replaced by the power of standards that transcend borders, standards that are more fragmented and decentralized, competing with samples and populations whose practices do not resemble each other, and on which a mode of harmonization is imposed that completely eludes legitimate states. The problem is that, outside the jurisdiction of a State, the norm appears more and more as a standardization imposed by interest groups, groups of influence whose subject is not easy to perceive, whose visibility no longer passes through institutions but perhaps through tentacular companies, living off migration, banking on the misery of stateless people. But the interplay of norms takes place at much more insignificant levels, in the everyday space of consumer goods and foodstuffs. Production and manufacturing methods may be subject to standards, as in the case of labels such as "label bio" or "label de qualité supérieure", but if they are designed in France, they no longer have a place of origin, which is impossible to control, as the components are assembled in a way that includes countries such as China, whose standards are anything but "bio". For this very reason, political management and consumer protection specifications are becoming ineffective, leaving the way open for uses that give cause for concern in terms of health. Standards do not meet the same thresholds of tolerance and visibility. What is true of the world of consumption obviously applies to the world of people, to community life, where many *regularities* intertwine, and where constraint is no longer political. Faced with this vacuum of the State, with the place left vacant, religious consumption practices are unleashed, rituals are over-coded, and uncivilized forms of demand are made to normalize the way we consume as much as the way we dress or meet.

It's hard not to see the bankruptcy of institutions everywhere. So, if there is to be a return to politics, there is no guarantee of the nature of this return, which could certainly give way to the brutality of totalitarian states, as is currently visible in certain regions of the world where everything has to be ritualized. And even in Europe, if the return of the State is still sometimes felt, it's not through the expression of the interests of the people, but through a particular twist, a security mesh around the territory, conflicts abroad, growing threats between Putin, Obama, Merkel and Hollande that maintain the allure of a declaration of war. This fortification of the State on the international stage, this external representation of the ultimately most powerless players, accompanied by vague NGOs with humanitarian aims, only serves to neglect domestic politics, the lives of the people threatened by the greed of the privileged and the rapacious behavior of white-collar criminals. To give the Regency a lost authority, the State is left with the otherwise violent figure of the demagogue, exerting his power externally through war, and internally by circulating fear in the form of intimidation, which seems to be the only weapon left to authenticate the figure of the politician. So we accuse each other of imaginary crimes that will become the slogans of the moment. Intellectuals are called upon to validate a policy, demanding a way of thinking that embraces lost causes without any critical exercise[31].

So we're no longer in the situation of Marx's division into well-defined classes to play the game of historical dialectics. This is no doubt because we have left the age of matter, of materialism, and entered the age of *dematerialization*. Social formations" are no longer characterized by the dualism of "classes" - an artificial, clear-cut dualism, when we reason in terms of populations and norms. The latter, in fact, have become indistinguishable, interweaving several layers of power: a set of normative games that intersect to gain in efficiency or, on the contrary, cancel each other out in an invasive, cancerous form. Beyond this complexion of clashing norms, we can see the same "subject" passing through different populations in which he will not have the same identity, taking on different names, according to different social networks, remaining anonymous in one, pseudonymous in another, or identifiable in a third by virtue of a headquarters, a religion, a social function, a company he infects or may sell, bankrupt, etc. Bernard Tapie was the name of Adidas before he was the name of a "Ministère de la Ville" or a TV show in a displacement that increased his power, always on the verge of collapse. And in the face of the rise of these heteronymous identities, the State is disappearing. It is caught up, electorally caught up, by the power of communication. It enters into the partisan service of those

---

31. The tension between Onfray and Valls is significant in this respect.

who ensure its election, and who have nothing to do with the people. In return, it will serve to spread these networks of power, which will absorb legislation that has become normative and European for groups capable of living outside real territories, of parasitizing them, connected to the international systems of global finance. We could imagine the implementation of a network, recently criticized by Junker, "President of the European Commission", which would have given very large companies the possibility of tax exemption and of finding channels to Luxembourg to avoid taxation in Europe, by creating the means of this invisibility through a skilful interplay of standards[32]. The State is thus reduced to rubble through incessant leaks, and can no longer protect us from predation. All those whose influence does not reach an image capable of giving them credit are counted as insignificant, those who remain bogged down in a territory, in a fiefdom, reproached for immobilism, lack of flexibility, a rootedness that would cost too much... The State finds itself overwhelmed, deposed by the international processes of unbridled capitalism, as we can see in the case of the Greek people, who are going to have to come into conflict with the demands of the economy, of a debt whose interest rates exceed the repayment capacity of a nation, while the slightest company that goes bankrupt sees its slate wiped clean. Here are the Greeks, inexorably faced with an original sin that is impossible to reset, and which will be borne by future generations.

---

32. Cf. *Huffington Post*, November 6, 2014.

The State no longer appears as the expression of the ruling class. It is no longer an instrument of domination, but becomes a legal entity incurring a debt that can never be paid off. And in a space in debt, the only resource is to transform the smallest citizen into a consumer force, in order to get growth going again. Being a citizen will become nothing more than a potential consumer, credible to the extent of the credit granted. Indebtedness affects everyone in the form of a new figure we might call the consumer, as consumption is now the sole reason for work, with shopping and shop windows as the sole purpose of activity. Everyone becomes a consumer to a certain extent and in certain ways, even the company director who consumes information. Successive heads of state present themselves as shopkeepers who travel with Medef to sell combat aircraft, nuclear power plants or high-speed trains abroad. In this sense, the state is used as a store, or even as a relic, becoming a ghost that no longer has the means to govern anything. Junker put it very well when he said that a democratic process, such as the election of a new government in Greece, "cannot modify" the decisions of the European economy and "the decrees of its treaty", since any policy is reduced to the commodification of the people[33].

For all these reasons, the State, normally representative of the common interest, takes on the image of an absent guarantor, giving way to strange powers, to partisan upsurges relaying through faith or morality a normativity

---

33. Interview with President Junker given to *Le Figaro* on January 29, 2015, in which he rejects the proposals of the new Greek government.

that increasingly eludes the law. It is as if the law no longer had any initiatives other than the purely technical ones of guaranteeing the European treaty or encouraging the dismantling of national industries in deregulated areas. Everything is managed for the benefit of a market that dreams only of relocation, of breaking down the laws in force in a given nation. Justice is being challenged, and the impoverishment of institutions is reaching alarming levels. At the same time, politics loses its regulatory function by losing the Law, by losing the Idea that serves as its guiding thread, abandoning all ideals denounced as ideological. And we applaud with both hands, calling on intellectuals to proclaim the death of ideologies in favor of technocratic management, far more bureaucratic than in the past. The mechanisms protecting people from predation are gradually being destroyed, and public services are being denounced as a luxury incompatible with profitability. The State, in the name of governance, of what we used to call *Regency*, is in the process of deregulating all social protections, of "setting the course", of "taking measures" that "go in the right direction", to use the Prime Minister's sanctimonious vocabulary. This is a Regency that can no longer maintain any protection, any security, the word security having no other meaning than that of microsurveillance, of the target to be offered up to the public to suggest a return to politics and its coercive force. All the barriers against corruption demanded by the people are constantly being dismantled under the impetus of laws like Macron's, on the grounds of their cost. In this way, the State promotes the elements of

its own destruction, placing itself under the high authority
of Brussels, which demands that social protections be
reduced. As a result, the exercise of power is increasingly
confined to a few illusory operations, military stunts to
demonstrate authority. And the new measures promised
by the Right, short of ideas, will be those of greater police
and judicial efficiency. But what this authority covers are
mechanisms to protect the transfer of currency, the relocation of tax-financed businesses, and so on.

Everything else in the public arena seems like a useless
weight to be rid of, an anti-virus to be knocked down by
forms of infection, Trojan horses that the state is willing to
harbor. Laws are still effective, but their legality has shifted
to a normative space that seizes on eloquent examples to
hide others, on major collective affairs to remake its image.
A normativity that seeks above all to take immediate action,
to multiply in the face of the news, the visible facts that cover
up more insidious ones. Normativity of this kind has become
more insidious than the Law, the rule, the regulation of
predatory practices. The freedom to enjoy, the great freedom
of the individual in the face of the State claimed by all the
new rich post-Sixties, has been deregulated into a form of
unbridled free enterprise, with no fiscal counterpart. It is
undoubtedly those who demanded the most enjoyment in
the '68s who today unabashedly grant it to themselves by
destroying the law, the Labor Code, which stood in the way of
their desire to exploit and propagate their viruses. The state is
no longer seen as self-evident, nor as something oppressive
in itself that can be identified and posed as an enemy. There's

no need to fight against the state or against what remains of justice in the regulation of human affairs. The State destroys itself under the usurping Regency. It is itself that is lost, that is losing itself by adopting the form of technocratic governance, governance that no longer concerns the people. The withering away of the democratic State is no longer simply the victory dreamed of by communism, but a bankruptcy orchestrated by "ideological-economic" norms, those of purely instrumental governmentality at the service of the globalized economy.

The withdrawal of the political and the legal into the background of European directives leads to a strange subject. A production of "self" as a commodity, and commodities as "self", whose subjection takes on an anonymous form, impossible to detect due to computer processing, due to the dematerialization of addresses and networks. It's as if the modern subject has been transformed into a listing, a history that degenerates it into a mere product (a data record known as *Big Data*). "I" has become a standardized subject, a commodity that "therefore I am" as a consumable consumer. In such a mutation, there is a standardized subjugation by powerful algorithms, not only with the idea of producing *hyperconsciousness,* as the recent Google project[34] aims to do, but to transform "subjects" into data, a data journey, a consumption journey in which they themselves become a marketable commodity, identically reproduced

---

34. Barbara Cassin, *Google-moi*, Paris, Albin Michel, 2007, who foresees the normativity at work in the "me" emerging from this virtual space.

and recognized around slogans that demand that we align ourselves with the same communication strategies. "I" is not a subject who thinks, but "I am Charlie" without even having to choose it, suspecting if need be of not adhering to the logo of a commodification that associates all the representatives of Europe. Such an observation makes it difficult to identify this anonymous agent with a class, to set proletarians against presumed bourgeois, knowing that the subjects have changed, impossible to detect, to refer to an interest that is truly political. In our resistance, as in our possible identifications, we have become *transclasses*.

Transclasses

The concept of *transclasses* was proposed by Chantal Jacquet in a book of the same name[35]. It is written in the plural because it does not refer to a particular class, but to a hydrid form, a form that contains a plurality of individuals who do not belong to the same edge, to the same gender. It's a question of modes of existence that don't fit into any single category, thereby escaping social reproduction, the reproduction of an identifiable type: worker, intellectual, boss. The tendency to categorize the social field according to watertight units has a long tradition. It can already be seen in Plato, when he distinguishes in an ideal city between those who govern and those who work or practise martial arts, not to mention much later in the Middle Ages, when he invented the category of those who pray. But this determinism of

---

35. Chantal Jaquet, *Les transclasses ou la non-reproduction*, Paris, PUF, 2014.

quasi-hereditary social reproduction, dependent on transmission and filiation, is already questionable under Roman law, and its Empire, when a slave can become a free man, or even, like Epictetus, a friend of the emperor[36]. There's a plasticity to social functions that doesn't sit well with castes and classes. Defectors have always played a decisive role, opening up the frontiers of the imagination, thwarting barriers and compartmentalization. Literature has made them a heroic resource, with Jean Valjean and the Count of Monte Cristo crystallizing popular utopias based on hybrid figures. A mythical porosity that the contemporary world now accentuates in a more trivial way, a wandering that no longer fits into any framework or under any regulations. Deregulation and flexibility are leading to the deregulation of society itself, with its divisions, insurances and guarantees. We change jobs and functions according to the needs of the market, and the word "competence" covers trans-disciplinary mobility rather than specific know-how.

Chantal Jaquet's treatment of the transclass is akin to Stendhal's Julien Sorel in *The Red and the Black, who* crosses the watertight walls that divide society between those who hold the keys to success and those who have nothing. With the risk, however, of ending up downgraded, losing his status as a subject, uprooted from any standardized existence, on the verge of pathology. The modern subject is certainly no longer one whose passions illuminate the divisions of reason, the respect of a class conscience. And it's certainly

---

36. He enjoyed the respect of Hadrian and the admiration of Marcus Aurelius.

no longer the mythical reference to the Roman Empire, whose space implies travel and mobility, that can help us grasp this wandering. Nor is it the chivalric figure of the man who sets off in search of himself, to conquer a voyage of initiation. The figure of success no longer has anything to do with a quest (*queste*), a "question", an interrogative form of self-concern. Success is more a question of the speed of development in the field of data, in *Big Data*, which enables us to identify trends through digital memory, even before they are realized. Events in globalization are anticipated by sampling. And in a sampling, the speed of action suddenly sees the emergence of the new rich, incredibly rich, with the perpetual risk of collapse, and the poor who cannot enter the information network, unless they enter from the margins, by *hacker* tinkering. In this gaseous context, one or other hero of the day can make his mark with a resounding *buzz*, thereby capitalizing on fortunes without any historical awareness or rules of action rooted in the slower movements of tradition. Once again, this leads to rapid change and an instability that is not underpinned by any founding thought or even habit. Value is now suspended on a mode of exploitation that is sensitive only to the microseconds that the computer grasps. The *dematerialization of* values can no longer be thought of in terms of historical *materialism*. Matter has evaporated. As a result, capital is no longer human. It imposes a speed that has gone mad. Through mobility and the constant changing of hats, references are exploding. The caste society has thus been pulverized at the crossroads of experiences that make it impossible for subjective identity to rest in itself.

The novelty of usage, the ongoing revolution in styles and codes for writing, informing and communicating, lead the modern subject to take on the figure of the transclass, with its dazzling successes and foretold downfalls. Each individual is carried like a dice, like the throw of a dice with its share of chances and misfortunes, with no guarantee of success thanks to training, or even a prestigious school to establish it, enthroning it according to the prestige of a caste, as in the case of successful HEC alumni who guarantee the support of younger students through a kind of feudal bond. The exception is now the rule for those who can guarantee themselves a success that owes nothing to anyone, without faith or law, a free rider if ever there was one, but who owes everything to the recognitions between which he plays the defector. With the perpetual risk of occupying a place that is not his own, of being displaced, of feeling his position as different from the one he should legitimately occupy, between glory and shame. The promise is gone. We've probably stopped making promises based on a clearly defined *curriculum*. Success is not a matter of law or faith. It's a journey.

In this respect, the conditions of existence of the contemporary subject will be those of the pseudonym, perpetually foreign, placed under new languages that impose themselves, too old or sometimes too young for the tools it manipulates, for the information of its own value, its own price. Transclasses are part of this competitive logic of the *link*, in the sights of "search engines" and "headhunters", not knowing whether their head will be put at a price, will fall, whether the guillotine will pass through the cleaver of revolution or reputation. The result is a fluctuating relationship with oneself, with the image that defines us, leading us into a perpetual vertigo.

Unable to stabilize their own vision of themselves, the transclasses experience the wanderings of globalization as if in an empire where movement is synonymous with success as much as decline. There is no longer any path traced by a curriculum, whether at school, the grandes écoles or university. Nothing is guaranteed by a diploma, by a "certificate of studies" as we used to say after the war. Studies no longer "certify" any path in the probabilistic space of globalization. Every career path is experienced as being ahead of its time, with a perpetual downgrading of our potential and our value, which has become purely virtual, a function of a hunt and a profile that happens in the hour, in short-term profitability. A subject's value, subjectivation and recognition depend on the *kilo-links* he or she is able to display on Twitter. It's through the indication of these links, through the number of associations, that the subject gains volume. He himself becomes a line in a sample, either through the number of virtual friends or the portfolio of recognitions that LinkedIn is striving to professionalize. And as these links consolidate or disintegrate, we can perhaps expect to see those in their fifties who are judged to be competent by their titles being thrown out of work. Communication may even come into play in retirement for individuals whose contributions have been promising, but who have nothing to offer in terms of influence, unable to reinvest their earnings in the stock market. Only shareholders can still claim a pension.

Ultimately, deregulation affects the mode of existence of those who can no longer inscribe themselves in the present, who no longer carry any form of advice, any informative resources, any capacity to radiate in the space of links. To the point of finding an ineffaceable signature, perhaps in a tattoo or piercing.

This is the time of the world, of the present moment, which sees itself as being placed at the pinnacle of history, with the past and future justifying nothing more than the narrowness of a path between norms. The contemporary subject, envisaged as transclass, could resemble the silver surfer, hero of an American comic strip who knows how to fit in nowhere, a stranger to every land, downgraded in every place. But this "surfing" is played out on the Web, leaving traces, *cookies* in search engines, in a frequented Facebook account, measurable by the quality of the friends who carry it or abandon it and to whom the *debts* become infinite, never enough to pay their gratitude. He is placed in the erratic solitude of the blogger, which lends his soul a desperate, exasperating instability, with the duty of promoting something new every day. In this respect, we're always in a perilous situation, on the periphery of a world we've just left, and a world we have to integrate through new debts. It's a perpetual process of refoundation, based on the collapse of acquired foundations. This produces a distance from everything - distance from the world we've just moved into, and distance from the universe we've just left behind, perpetual distraction, daze - all of which characterize those who no longer belong to any class, on the periphery of all environments crossed.

The *stranger*, the Web surfer, the one who zaps sites as much as classes, ultimately belongs nowhere, loses all *habitus*, all habitation and all *ethos*, all ethics. No doubt this gesture will have something of the heroic about it, as the heroes of *Strange magazine* showed in their day. What debts have they contracted to feel obliged to save humanity? We can certainly detect virtues, mutations and metamorphoses that contemporary philosophy is constantly questioning, from Deleuze to Derrida. Philosophers who question nomadism as a response to capitalism, to this world from which we must extract new weapons to defend ourselves and assert our rights. Resistance to the enslavement of capitalism cannot come from a way of thinking that reclaims the old philosophy of the subject, closed in on itself, reasoning in terms of foundation, foundation, territory. But it's not without being constantly captured by systems that seek to burden you with unsuspected, moral debts, treating those who move as *products*. Displacement and migration are movements that capitalism will use as means of production, whose capitalization we should be able to denounce and criticize, as Deleuze does in *Capitalism and Schizophrenia*, when capitalism is linked to the mental decline of the psychotic subject, cleaved by worlds that absorb, divide and detach him from his creative possibilities, through a market that taps into the force of displacement, turning nonsense into a mode of production, a reterritorialization through indebtedness. This is a form of machine capture, an arrangement that extracts information value from every transfer of the subject, every move on the Web: a trajectory that makes him carry new pots and pans, new cookies[37]. This great divide between so many different worlds, constantly crossed by transclasses in planes and geolocated cars, leads the subject to a form of extreme profitability, but through subterranean contradictions that make his life hell. Such nomadism can produce a space of freedom for a subject who can transform the overflight of environments into a mode of existence, but the problem comes from the fact that it's not so much he who projects and constructs himself, realizes himself as such, but the conditions to which he submits himself and which will turn him into an indebted wreck offering his body to society. A bit like the pitiful heroes of Alan Moore and Dave Gibbons' *Watchmen*, who pursue a strange *smiley* face icon that we all use. The "subject" of this decaying world is embodied by the main character, Rorschach, who can only exist by changing his features, his mask, at every moment and in every environment he crosses.

There's no turning back. History is not happening in reverse. We are indeed in the age of cybernetic techniques, of a planetary form of "deterritorialization", of delocalization, to which it would make no sense to oppose a communist hypothesis based on classes and castes from another age. But this *stranger*'s mode of existence, this downgraded life, philosophy can think of it in the creative form that corresponds to it, rejecting debt, the figure of the indebted man. We can no longer dream of the immobility of a society set

---

37. Such machinations are described by Gilles Deleuze and Félix Guattari in *L'Anti-Œdipe*, Paris, Éditions de Minuit, 1972.

in the substance of tradition, in the stability of its order, its unchanged nature. The fact that God is dead means we can no longer dream of new gods, as the process has become irreversible. Everything is constantly being undone and remade, in a kind of trance that has accelerated. The bankruptcy of today's capitalism brings with it a world to come, the profile of which we are still struggling to grasp, a world for which we still lack the forms of a corresponding state, a policy for a society that is nonetheless already here, in all its contradictory dynamics. The time is ripe for the variation of a processual society, a society as it might be thought from Deleuze onwards, a society that can no longer rely on identifiable subjects, nor on the unchanging evidence of a national map, as if frozen by a label. Some animals are capable of varying their color, of shedding an old skin for new mimesis. So it is with societies, and Greek communism is unlikely to be comparable with a policy that relies on the identical reproduction of patterns that even Chinese communism has abandoned. So, for a subject of this kind to free itself from the machinations of banking and financial capture, it presupposes, at the very least, an analysis of their mechanisms and modes of resistance that we have yet to explore. The end of history is certainly not for today.

III/ The Savagery of Capitalism

The Morality of Debt

There is no economic crisis. It's not the economy that's in crisis, but the states that are subject to it[38]. The economy is doing as well as it could ever have dreamed, demanding in the imposition of its law and the logic of debt, which it exploits in a way that Nietzsche called moral when, in the 19th century, he set out to show that all morality finds its genealogy in the denunciation of debt. And things like this don't change overnight. In the second essay of *La généalogie de la morale*, Nietzsche opens fire with a clear statement. He speaks of "breeding an animal that can promise"[39]. This is what makes morality inseparable from an economy. And to

---

38. On this point, we refer to Maurizio Lazzarato's analysis, *Gouverner par la dette*, Paris, Les Prairies ordinaires, 2014, which evokes Joseph Stiglitz's observation concerning the richest 1%, "le gouvernement du 1% pour le 1%, par le 1%", p. 23.

39. Nietzsche, *La généalogie de la morale* (The Genealogy of Morals), Œuvres, Gallimard, vol. VII, p. 251.

understand this, we need look no further than the German language, where *debt* and *morality* have become consubstantial. Indeed, *Schuld* (meaning "fault" in the moral sense) is embedded in the financial concept of *Schulden*, which means "debts", "indebtedness", as if punishment, moral retribution, were associated with the expiation of a debt, linked to the contractual relationship between *creditor* and *debtor*[40]. How could such a contract come into being? Is it possible to accept such an imbalance? Is it so difficult to understand such a humiliating contract? Breaking a contract was, Nietzsche tells us quite simply, an act that made the one who broke it a damned man, a man eternally indebted, banished, rejected, excluded, so that "the abused creditor will always be repaid"[41]. This is what "redemption" means, the act of making amends, of being "bought", economically speaking, for those who break their promise. The one who becomes a "sold out", must sell himself in return, become a slave or carry the world on guilty shoulders.

The creditor is immediately in the position of master, by the simple act of giving, by the bewitching virtue of the gift. Charity is an ambiguous act, not only to mark one's superiority, but also to create indebted men and women. The creditor creates. He creates unlimited dependence. In such a perspective, the discharge of debts is only apparent. Discharge of a debt could be envisaged when the objects exchanged were still commodities. Commodities are

---

40. *Ibid*, p. 257.
41. *Ibid*, p. 264.

material goods, especially for pawnbrokers. These goods have a prestige value that always exceeds the material from which they are made. Sometimes they are symbolic family heirlooms that make pawnbroking virtually unaffordable. But we find it impossible to pay when exchange becomes virtual, particularly in digital control societies. In this respect, we are indebted before we are born, carrying an infinite chain like the Greek people, whose debt will be transgenerational. And this guilt is already indexed in Kafka's work. "Kafka, who was already at the crossroads of two types of society, described the most formidable legal forms in *The Trial*: the apparent acquittal of disciplinary societies, the unlimited procrastination of control societies"[42]. The character "K" is guilty from birth, for no reason, through no fault of his own, in an absurd manner. It's hard to say exactly what the man who humiliates himself by going into debt is guilty of. When debt still took the material, objective form of usury and money, alienation could tolerate acquittal. Discharge remained possible for the borrower against the pawnbroker. But as soon as the object becomes codified and digitized, it loses all pledge. In the case of dematerialized goods, acquittal itself becomes unlimited. In Deleuze's words, "man is no longer a locked-in man, but an indebted man", "a man too poor for debt"[43]. We must therefore learn to be wary of giving, of organizations that lend, that give beyond all return something unpayable, essentially unpayable, and that disguise themselves under the guise of

---

42. Gilles Deleuze, "Post-scriptum sur les sociétés de contrôle" in *Pourparlers*, Éditions de Minuit, 1990, p. 243.
43. *Ibid*, p. 246.

Christian charity. It's up to the person who gets into debt to promise and keep that promise, even if it becomes infinite, as the demand for repayment is unconditional, pushing the person who contracts the debt to sell his body, if need be, his labor power to the hard service of another.

This fine analysis by Nietzsche, reread here by Kafka, explains better than Marx the workings of alienation and capitalist vampirization, even if Marx never ceased to denounce this spider that sucks the blood of its victim ("capital," he says, "only comes alive by sucking, like a vampire, living labor, which is all the more alive for sucking more of it"[44]). In any case, working for someone else doesn't just happen. You have to feel naturally enslaved, enslaved before God, affected by an original sin, a sin from before birth, a fault (*Schuld*) called debt (*Schulden*). How can such submission be explained? First and foremost, it could only be seen in the logic of the promise, a promise to return unconditionally what has been pledged: "it is precisely here that one promises; it is precisely here that it is a question of making a memory of the one who promises", according to a whole arsenal of humiliations that we continue to brandish today in Europe with regard to indebted countries. The logic of debt thus takes as its axiom the following formula: "Everything can be paid for, everything must be paid for"[45], even the unpayable. Paying the unpayable, as evidenced by the extortion of Greece's coastline by foreign creditors,

---

44. Karl Marx, *Capital*, ch. VIII, "The Working Day", Quadrige, PUF, 1993, p. 336.
45. Nietzsche, *op. cit.*, p. 265.

is considered a natural and moral folly by the Europeans who come to the peninsula's rescue, creating an image of charitable saviors. But what are these strange rescues and donations? There are debts linked to expenditure, of course. But there are proposals for toxic loans that have nothing to do with indebtedness. In fact, these proposals are based on the promise of added value, of an interest that we know can grow if we sell it. We can still promise the capital gain and sell the capitalization to buyers, buyers who are betting on the indebtedness of the States. It's clear to us that, in this kind of banking logic, work is uninteresting, and shareholders are no longer interested in the company and its resources in terms of jobs. "In the current situation, capitalism is no longer interested in production, which it often relegates to the periphery of the Third World [...], what it wants to sell are services, and what it wants to buy are shares [...]. Marketing is now the instrument of social control and forms the brazen breed of our masters.[46]"

Work, for such masters, is far too expensive, far too unprofitable for those who come to deregulate the law. Interest on debt, the indebtedness of a system, is financially far more promising than investment. In any case, debt repayment is not enough to mop up the immorality that dominates the course of the world. An immorality that imposes itself in the name of morality, of its entirely usurious and financial genealogy, as we have shown with Nietzsche. Debt repayment is not possible without the worldwide extortion to which

---

46. Gilles Deleuze, *op. cit.*, p. 246.

over-indulgent states fall victim, forced to lay off their agents to satisfy the kleptomania of the international financial system. Of course, the movement of wealth is increasingly dematerialized. Of course, since the French Revolution, land has no longer had a capitalizable value. Of course, the wealth of the subsoil has itself been relocated since the revolution of the "processing industries", which import their raw materials from undernourished countries. Of course - as we have amply analyzed - globalization itself has been relocating this processing to India and China for over two decades, and know-how is no longer considered an attractive "product" in the eyes of investors. In fact, "production" itself has become banking, indebted to a figure, a portfolio of shares that in the final analysis have nothing to do with assets... This is because the bank sees itself as the metaphysical locus of a productive concentration, a leftover, a poisoned remnant that is more interesting than investing in a company. It's like the return of the revenant, the ghost of all that dies, destroyed from within by debt. What prevails today is the spirit of a company, its form of communication, its signs and the shareholders it is capable of seducing. Spirit" is what remains when production is no longer material. The interest of the financial system, its spirit and its spectrum, lies in the creation of "financial products" that are more profitable than loans to companies, and necessarily more lucrative than investment in industrial or ecological resources, or in research[47]. At

---

47. It has to be said that in the United States, research is paramount, and costs companies far more than in France, where the main preoccupation of business leaders and those in power is the "exorbitant cost of labor".

worst, we're told, these worthy causes cost money, which could be much more profitable if applied without compensation to new nanomillimetre circulation modalities. Money is circulating crazier than ever. It has a limpid, metaphysical presence. More than ever, but less and less well distributed. It's so obvious, it's palpable in every survey that we don't even need to reproduce it. Everyone knows, and there's no need to misunderstand, as current events have shown all too well what cannot be ignored, to the point of becoming commonplace. We therefore subscribe to Deleuze's formula: "In capitalism, there is only one thing that is universal, and that is the market. There is no universal state, precisely because there is a universal market, of which states are the focal points, stock exchanges.[48]"

The City of God

The State has lost its universality to capitalist ecumenism. The reality of globalization has led to the implementation of financial procedures capable of capturing wealth at the expense of labor, at the expense of human resources. Consumption itself is no longer essential for those who feed on highly dematerialized money, pursued for its witchcraft, for its immateriality. The rich aren't just stingy. They essentially don't need money. It's the poor who need to pay for the services provided by works councils with executive cars, parking spaces, overheads, severance pay and parachutes.

---

48. Gilles Deleuze, "Contrôle et devenir" in *Pourparlers* (Paris: Éditions de Minuit, 1990), pp. 229-239, *loc. cit.* pp. 233-234.

Access codes are all it takes to open Sesame's doors. This ethereal circulation embodies a form of sanctity that doesn't need to show its currency. The creation of poverty enables us to attach ourselves to the world's indebted, to enslave them, to give them a grade and subject them to our law. The triple AAA rating is an invention of the kleptomania of the financial markets, which thus find a way to aggravate the bankruptcy of states. Instead of investing in human action, finance feeds on the austerity it imposes because it will be extremely profitable in the short term, because it brings more pleasure than any other good. To be seen and desired by those who have nothing is an incomparable pleasure. The money that Europe lends to Greece is obviously not at all for the Greeks, and will immediately go back to the banks, which will receive the interest directly and numerically. The fact that the whole of Europe finds itself rated by an agency of magicians and conjurers (who are they?) shows just how haunted we are by the metaphysical illusions that Marx was already denouncing with regard to market value and the scenic processes of commodification. It's all about the stage. There is no "cleptocracy", as Sloterdijk's very interesting analysis too quickly suggests. It's not the States that are suffocating us with taxes at all, but the financial agencies that are indulging in kleptomania by pushing up pharaonic interest rates that annually exceed the budget allocated to the Ministry of Research - a veritable manna from heaven. And to make this miracle even greater, to impose increasing austerity capable of diverting the wealth of salaries to creditors, all we have to do is lower this rating to increase the debt, thus recovering the money that no longer goes to public companies, this money useless to those who, in any case, would never work enough, protected by labor laws, regulations that are increasingly perceived as a scandal, denounced everywhere. The demand for rules at work is soon perceived as a delinquent attitude... It has always been necessary for work to atone for divine punishment.

Deleuze and Guattari were exemplary in foreseeing the miraculous nature of capitalism. Jean-Louis Schefer, however, is responsible for the historical demonstration, as if capitalism were nourished by a theological unconscious, by a faith in capital that sought to be scientific while ignoring the mysticism that underpins it. Historically, the mass production of money is not unrelated to theophany. Moulds for money are the same as those for hosts, as if money were to conquer a glorious body, as early as the 11th century, when hosts were made "in the shape of money"[49]. It's the same process that places silver in the odor of sanctity. It is immaculate in the manner of the lamb. Gold is minted in the likeness of the redeeming lamb. This would seem to be a form of mystical valuation of money, a convergence of money and holiness, as if to lead the circulation of wealth towards a supernatural life, a desire placed at the birth of capitalism, washed away by the debts contracted by the damned. But this idealization of its now so volatile price also intertwines money with other forms of incorporeal value, with other modes of decorporation, of dematerialization, which we can enumerate in bulk:

---

49. Jean-Louis Schefer, *L'hostie profanée*, Paris, P.O.L., 2007.

1° In the 12th century, money and its minting became polarized around saintly figures, and in particular relics, which were constantly moved in procession. The cult of relics allowed money to flow like a bank, promising immortal interest. Money is polarized around the presence of saints, who carry the residual interest into another life. You're buying your eternal life, as it were. And the relic is miraculous, giving way to immortality. But in return, it generates an infinite debt that cannot be paid, except by committing all one's energies to building the holy place. In a way, paradise is rented at this time, and a second life is bought with the money donated to the holy places. From this point onwards, witchcraft was denounced as a form of acquittal with regard to a claim that had become mystical. But it's the relic that takes on the function of exchange and turns the economy into a form of prodigality of the saint, a holy currency, a holy effigy.

2° For all these reasons, the saint's relic polarizes the attractive wealth of a region, allowing it to "radiate" through a reputation, a new, intangible value that reflects on economic life. It is the host of nascent capitalism, with flows, anointings, the holy unction, the transport of vials that corporates crowds like a shroud capable of spreading oil, by contact, imprint, odor of sanctity, etc. The translation of relics attracts around it the wealth of a region, which is thus able to "radiate" through a reputation, a new, immaterial value, which reflects on economic life. The transfer of relics attracts money through promises and speculation on insolvent debts. In this way, it makes it possible to redeem our faults without any other than supernatural repayment, *redeeming* our sins in a certain sense, which is the basis of Cluny's wealth.

3° Value follows the movement of peregrination polarized by the relic. Hence the immense relocation of pilgrimages, and the "peace of God" movements that assert their right, putting all reality in crisis. What circulates is the host as currency, behind the redemption of eternal life, behind the tabernacle of teeth, shins, nails, hair, dried blood, a kind of Brownian movement of relics. Vézelay, for example, builds a tax haven by carrying on its back the remains of the city of Aix, destroyed by the Saracens, and from which it inherits a relic: the supplement, what remains of the remains of Aix. A fragment carries with it an incredible array of legends constituting the West as a "city of God".

4° Roman law had already "functionalized" or instrumentalized bodies to make them part of larger entities, such as property, or even larger entities such as the Empire. The slave thus becomes part of the property, a cog in the wheel, an uprooting from his organs subjected to the *outside*, to the law that cuts them up and punishes by ripping out his tongue if need be. The surgery of codes and the suffering of debt. I believe that this debt, which reduces the body to the state of a *sign*, is the mainspring of Nietzsche's *Genealogy of Morals*, which is a semiology of bodies marked by debt.

5° It's likely that Foucault's unpublished book, *Aveux de la chair*, is along the same lines. The body, through this integration into a larger machine, is no longer quite matter, of the order of *res*, substance. It becomes a function. Hence the importance of civil servants, of the citizen who receives an annuity, a property from the emperor, and so on. Under the name of function, the body is taken as part of an abstract machine that Deleuze calls a "body without organs". It is the life of the mind. It is cut up to redeem debts by integrating itself under different machines and relocations forming the complete virtualization of public space. In the Christian universe, the body of Christ is no longer the body of Jesus, but that of an immense social machine that is supposed to unite Christians: Christendom, an economic and ecumenical body.

6° The body of Christ, which merges with Europe, has been deterritorialized into something as abstract as the chalice, the transportable, invasive currency. The body of Christ, in the host, is effectively dematerialized and diffused in the currency mode. But it seems to me that it is the relic that forms its capiton, its point of capitalization, its wealth, the promise of a divine city, of an abstract body as new matter. Fragments without substratum that give Europe a glorious body, as if its territory needed this fragment to find its frontier and embody itself in states that would be subject to it[50].

The Sanction of AAA Ratings

The relic not only established a holy place, but also functioned as a pole of attraction, a magnet for wealth from lands sometimes far away. It overflows its territory. It promises interest, a residue, a surplus value that subsists in a similar

---

50. We developed this analysis of the Middle Ages in *Ossuaire - une anatomie du Moyen Âge roman*, Paris, Payot, 1995.

form in the witchcraft of capitalism. Capitalism lives on remnants, *relics*, relics of the imaginary that polarize the capture of surplus value, through the growing globalization of finance and the creation of miraculous "financial products" that inevitably lead us to a "Banking International"[51]. It's an International whose markets are based on laundered networks that escape the control of temporal power. And the banking network, immaculate by design, will quickly refuse to apply the liberalism it now imposes on the ECB. As soon as it comes to rescuing the banks, liberalism is out of the question, and taxes are called in to limit the damage. In this paradoxical perspective, it is the citizens who will be mobilized to "save the banks", as the presidency had made its motto. So we're advocating liberalism in the way we make profits, while curiously reserving a communism of principle, a certain mutuality to impose the right to puncture our savings books if need be. This is the height of debt, when taxes are used to allocate money at zero interest, which is then reinjected into the most speculative credit cycle. Whereas competition used to be supposed to regulate financial markets, the banking system, now global, is no longer subject to competition as it dangles pharaonic loans to states for which it has become impossible to repay loans at the rate defined by the sovereignty of a people. All it would take is the political will - or at least a return to the noble meaning of the word "political" - to

---

51. Here we agree with some of David Graeber's intuitions from other perspectives that do not adopt his model of a *universal history that is,* so to speak, still too monumental, cf. *Dettes 5000 ans d'histoire*, Paris, Éditions Les liens qui libèrent, 2013.

III/ The Savagery of Capitalism

untangle this speculative hydra and dismantle this klepto-maniacal and prophetic association.

In this respect, we urgently need to rethink our banking services and get away from the "miracles" of the economy. We need to return to banks that can play a useful role, and recreate the conditions for credit that serves companies and people. The Greek people - to whom we owe the idea of politics - don't seem to have succeeded in doing this, having, we are told, spent lavishly. Nor did the Italians measure the impact of the efforts demanded of them by Mario Monti, Prime Minister (2011-2013) and former member of the *subprime-friendly* Goldman Sachs bank, which was fined $5 billion in April 2016 for its role in the 2008 real estate crisis. The French are waiting to see what nectar they will be intoxi-cated with, pushed to a threshold of tolerance that could well reawaken the battles of its history, which we all know is not over, that it will have to get rid of the demands of Brussels to rethink even its security, that of Europe itself, which has virtually no means left to defend itself, deemed too costly.

No doubt we should be astonished and scandalized when the far right topples a government here or there. But that's forgetting that these governments were proposing the pure application of an ultraliberal clause, that of raising VAT, freezing wages and cutting jobs, as if European politics were now sacrificing its entire future to a debt whose profit now only satisfies the empire of finance, thought of as the "city of God". Remember that in 2014, Standard & Poor's threatened to downgrade Argentina's credit rating for not complying with debt requirements. But all's well that ends well, as

Christina Kirchner's successor as Argentine president, once elected, rushed to reimburse the American vulture funds that were pursuing Argentina with the support of the rating agencies and the US justice system. Yet this was a debt for which the interest ultimately culminated in the name of no public use, of no purpose, but solely in the name of the very sanctity of the monetary host and its ultracapital moral law... It's remarkable that we can be scandalized by an effect alone when the causes are to be found elsewhere. Households obliged to allocate all their meagre earnings to consumption, the total consumers we have become, whose entire salaries are spent on basic necessities, will be taxed at 18% and more, insofar as misfortune may lead them to consume alcohol or tobacco, not to mention highly-taxed petrol or the delirious price of so-called personal loans designed to survive, weighed down by unbridled compulsory insurance. Add to this indirect tax the direct tax, however negligible, which severely affects low-income earners and the middle classes. These are all sectors that will be held hostage by cumulative levies that could exceed 50% of their incomes, at a time when the richest are defiscalising tax in their droves, always scandalized by the fact that they are the only ones working. It's not the most underprivileged who escape taxes levied directly at the time of purchase, which are heavier to bear when you have little. The problem is that this money is no longer used for public space, where even the benches are bristling with uncomfortable structures: instruments of torture to dissuade people from using them, to prevent them from resting. There's nothing to be gained from public space, except through abusive taxation of toilets, some of which are scandalously inaccessible, stitched together with gold and white thread. Instead of contributing to the common good, the windfall from these activities goes straight into debt, bailing out the artificial havens of speculation.

The Metaphysical Illusion of Capitalism

That the only liberal morality lies in repaying a debt that imposes itself on the whole of Europe as a "categorical imperative" is hardly debatable. Like any categorical imperative, the sanctity of its law will never be debated in the real world of European politics. Debt is the a priori form of policies born of a long religious history, according to which man may think of his apocalypse. And as soon as a policy deviates from this requirement to make amends, which is presented to us as the only possible redemption, as soon as a protest is raised against this old idea of debt, whose ugly underbelly Nietzsche in his time had shown, the condemnation of the creditors will not be long in coming, and the resulting extreme behaviors will be singled out like a cardinal sin, a deviance or a heresy. This is not to say that we should accept and subscribe to such extremes. On the contrary, it's our duty to show that extremism and terror are a consequence of capitalism, of government by debt. Hence the importance of pointing to the extreme as a symptom. Is it not exacerbated capitalism that kills work and undermines lives locked in the guilt of infinite debt, an anhistorical debt that poisons the future and tomorrow's generations? No doubt we can rethink the category of gift and charity, as Peter Sloterdijk seems to want to do[52]. But how can we fail to see that charity is the prerogative of the rich, and debt is the hell of the poor? Should we not revisit the notion of debt as the burden of the humiliated and the original sin of their eternal guilt - all the more so since this expiatory category has now been adopted as the spearhead of global politics? How can we refuse to pay the debt, or even think about it lucidly, when we know the historical weight of this category around which Christianity was born, with the sacralization of volatile money, now incorporeal: a host mold infusing everywhere the mystical course of the stock markets, temples of modernity. The level of debt has reached such proportions that it now concerns a generation that has not contracted it, the generation of the future, whose inalienable right, it seems to us, lies in the ability to free itself from the past. There is no freedom when eternity becomes the monopoly of heirs or rentiers. The shadow cast by one generation over another renders unthinkable the emergence of the singular, of those who develop in the light of their own survival[53]. The seizure of the future by a generation of the past, the capitalization of the future, leads to the *bankruptcy of* democracy by projecting the errors and illusions of our unreasonable choices onto tomorrow's centuries.

Let's put it more complexly, in other words, more philo-sophically. Sanction generates sanction, and is amplified by its prescription and obedience. The globalization of financial

---

52. Peter Sloterdijk, *Repenser l'impôt*, Paris, Éditions Libella/Maren Sell, 2012.
53. On this alienation of singularity, cf. Marc Crépon, *Le discrédit de l'Europe*, lecture on Derrida reprinted by *Strass de la philosophie*, October 2014.

markets confers on rating agencies a supralunar location, the height of a "virtual locality" placed outside any political jurisdiction, sheltered by an absolute transcendence: a system whose perversity amounts to a new despotism. Great despots without politics (like all despots), who never live better than according to what we call a contradictory imperative (*double bind* or "double constraint"). The contradictory imperative is a rule according to which the situation worsens through obedience to what is prescribed. At the very moment of obeying it and for having obeyed it. Assuming that the demands of Standard & Poor's are heeded, the rout (or disemployment) would be such that growth would fall to unsustainable levels. With the absurd consequence of receiving a triple C for having taken this into account. As a result, interest rates on the debt would soar, satisfying the few "digital organizations" capable of profiting from it. Obeying the triple-A injunction would necessarily result in an even lower rating in the long term. For the simple reason that austerity weighs terribly on employment and wages, and makes all consumption problematic, thus making it possible to punish bad performers more severely. As a result, the latter will have to take on ever heavier debts, with ever more authoritarian interest rates. This vampire logic of financial rating leads to a veritable elevator leading parasites out of national political bodies, towards a heaven capable of making us endure its hell, any hell being the result of heaven dictating its law. As you can well imagine, this is an infernal spiral that can only glorify the interests of "speculation" against those of "production", traditionally linked to human action. The

AAA rating can only be satisfied by leading to the opposite of what was asked for. *Double bind* here means that if we were to subscribe to it, we would be severely sanctioned in return simply for having taken the initial injunction into account, which would trigger a new sanction. It's a spiral leading us towards a circle in which all rights are lost. This vicious circle of debt will inevitably lead to the collapse of capitalism itself.

The Negativity of Capitalism

The negativity of capitalism is on the verge of denying itself like a snake biting its own tail, but in a disappearance that risks taking with it everything humanity has created in terms of wealth and value, masterpieces and creations. We have no doubt that the birth of capitalism will have irrigated many creations, and that a city like Venice, a pure work of art, has benefited from the added value generated by the Silk Road, the route to the Orient, the transit of fabrics and rare goods, as if the merchant and the artist were congenitally linked, one taking from the multiplied wealth of the merchants what the other had the opportunity to make available through time freed from subsistence, freed from survival work, at first too crushed by natural necessities. Nor do we doubt the creations of metallurgy at the end of the 19th century by industrial companies that restructured a landscape through considerable public works, calling on technicians, engineers and, why not, philosophers. There is no such thing as a philosopher in a world whose only resource for existence is the sweat of our brows. We cannot naively give in to the victimization of those who blame civil society for their personal failure and defeat. We cannot indefinitely blame our failures on an aristocracy that liberates itself from work by making possible works that are indebted to the "noble leisure" of the intellect that Aristotle rightly called *Skholé*. But we are forced to recognize that the new productivity potentials of liberalism, the new purely financial investment sectors, are increasingly turning into destructive forces within the world that capitalism has subjected to its law, to the surge of its negativity and bankruptcy. A group like Wendel in France, historically linked to industry, has been transformed into a financial capture device, with catastrophic effects on companies, supposedly cleaned up and sold for their stock market value, but with no consideration for the people who work there.

We have to admit that greedy bankers have nothing in common with creation, and that profitability and creation have turned their backs on each other. There is no longer any real question of business creation. There's an unprecedented artificial inflation of the financial markets that has nothing to do with production, and which is sucking reality into unbridled speculation. As Lohoff and Trenkle understand, the third industrial revolution was still concerned with shaping material reality[54]. This revolution in material transformation could boast real effects, as it considerably reduced the number of unemployed workers in heavy industry. This corporate activity, which was not yet compared to a *mind*

---

54. Ernst Lohoff, Norbert Trenkle, *La grande dévalorisation*, Fécamp, Post-éditions, 2014.

capable of wooing shareholders, achieved beneficial results on innovative forms of work, making it possible to restrain the runaway pace of licensing. It has considerably slowed the accelerating eviction of labor power from the field of production. It protects us from the miraculous spheres of speculation. The industrial revolution, in all its forms, was supposed to keep capitalism in a real economy, in touch with matter, despite its inequalities and numerous injustices. But the surge of dematerialization is now inevitable, thanks to the massive recourse to credit and speculation, which play on delocalization and immaterial processes. Financial capitalism is speculation whose interests are linked to the unreal capture of time, the anticipated capture of future value. It thrives on transactions at infinite speed, made possible only by computers. These are all strategies based on fictitious promises, unleashed in the name of *belief*, as if every investment were a promised land.

It's a form of capitalism whose speculative bubbles are not based on any real production process, so that the 2008 crisis saw the system collapse, held together in extremis by the muscular intervention of central banks supported by compliant governments. The problem is that, since 2008, society has been living at a pace that is undoubtedly beyond what reality can offer in terms of materials and resources. All productivity potentials are in the red, and are inevitably turning into a destructive force. We may be living in a society that has become too rich, too rich for a "real economy", necessarily limited by the earth and the planet's resources. The immaterial modes of production that characterize the metaphysical system of finance are based on forms of wealth that matter cannot satisfy. These are forms of desire that are too delocalized, outside the boundaries of reality, of the possibilities and interests that life demands for its perpetuation. Today, we have reached the opposite of Bentham's proposition that liberalism would guarantee "the greatest happiness of the greatest number". It is the opposite proposition that is now the ultimate truth of a capitalism that destroys companies and dissipates into the nimbus of its utopia. There can be no financial "viability" in the knowledge that finance undermines life. We urgently need - as in the case of Iceland punishing its traders - to relocalize capitalism in the form of its material realization, and severely legislate against idealistic flights of fancy which, while turning away from reality, promise to vandalize and destroy it.

Some Ecosophical Perspectives

Capitalism obviously dreams of a stateless, totally deregulated society, with no power to intervene in the course of its interests. It's the implementation of a Regency that resists regulation by the political sphere. And this Regency bears no resemblance whatsoever to the revolutionary ideal which, according to Marxist-Leninist doctrine, would have overcome the State. Today, capitalism is no more than a name for the impoverishment of the planet, the end of a world that has nothing to do with technology, but with the choice of an energy model. Oil has been globalized by capitalism. It promotes the totalitarianism of "all oil". And nuclear power is just an extension of this. We always come back to a single, globally exploitable energy mode. It seems to me, on the contrary, that both oil and nuclear power are just one element in the technical scheme of things, and that there are an *infinite number of* others. Each energy has its own line of chaos, its own possible bomb, the outside world with which to contend. This is an unavoidable risk. No doubt we'll have to find a threshold that brings these energies into contact with other forms and frees them from the laws of finance. From a geographical point of view, renewable resources are specific to each case (aquatic, wind, solar, telluric). We therefore need to redeploy energy powers that are inappropriate in economic terms, but that are indebted to public space, to particular places capable of diversifying them. For the moment, we still don't pay for the air we breathe, and the same was true of water, fire and earth, considered as elements that belong to no one. Oil is a substance that is capitalized on in an utterly undignified way. And under the aegis of this capitalization, an all-powerful economy is imposed on us, that of the universalism of oil. On the contrary, it seems to me that biodiversity should be considered in terms of energies other than those that our economy has placed at the pinnacle of fiscal resources.

We know that mass fuel distribution will be a thing of the past in less than five decades' time, although there will of course be oil left over for strategic uses. What brought such a model to power, and who has an interest in maintaining it, on both the left and the right? What is the political explanation for the silence surrounding this inevitable change? How can we justify the desire to maintain the rights levied on this energy that excludes all others, impoverishing the various possible modes of production? There's a singular lack of diversity here, as our civilization has forgotten the use of the formidable machines that wind, sun and water made efficient, all financially inappropriate elements of sustainable activity. It's possible that nuclear power could be useful to us in fields yet to be defined, or that oil could be reserved for the conquest of space, providing us with the strength to escape gravity and set off to find other lands... It seems to me that we are living in interesting and rich times, if we take into account this mutation which is very close at hand, but which could degenerate into a planetary catastrophe if we continue to allow financiers to impose their conditions, their relocation frenzy snatching away all our know-how from the environments where they were born, for reasons of tax exemption and circumvented labor laws. What's on the horizon is an energy "pluriverse" that will bring us back into contact with matter through resources other than oil. And it's not the problem of democracy that's at issue, but rather the governance demanded by the markets, which appropriate the price of wheat and other vital energy commodities. On all these issues, the left says almost nothing. It's a politics that still lives in a world that's over, finished: the end of a world.

From my point of view, the future calls for a diversity of energies, an exploration of know-how other than that of the oil industry: steam, hydraulic, compressed air, light, wind, nanoworlds and cybernetics, which we won't be able to activate when we need to if we don't start thinking today about the way out of liberalism and its monocentric "universe" (which is hardly libertarian after all). For me, capitalism, which destroys all plurality, has nothing to do with enjoyment, as Slavoj Žizěk tends to think. Capitalism enjoys nothing, its enjoyment is impossible even through its relocations, and it knows neither ecstasy nor beatitude, caught only in the gray tightenings of what is exchanged, bartered, consumed and consumed. He is in the object that gives him the illusion of a glorious body through the destruction of matter. We'd do much better to reread Spinoza for a true idea of beatitude, and to imagine from there what expenditure and enjoyment, power and creation mean, in a nature that he wants to be "naturante", infinitely extendable, modulable according to inexhaustible forms.

From the Same Author

Essays:

Variations. The Philosophy of Gilles Deleuze, Payot, 1993 (paperback ed., 2005)

Ossuaires. Anatomie du Moyen Âge roman, Payot, 1995

L'Image virtuelle. Essai sur la construction du monde, Kimé, 1996

L'Âme du monde. Availability of Aristotle, Les Empêcheurs de penser en rond/Seuil, 1998

Van Gogh. L'œil des choses, Les Empêcheurs de penser en rond/Seuil, 1998

L'opposition universelle, Preface to Gabriel Tarde, Les Empêcheurs de penser en rond/Seuil, 1999

François Rouan. Papiers découpés, Somogy Éditions d'Art, 2000

Figures des temps contemporains, Kimé, 2001

Parures d'Éros. Un traité du superficiel, Kimé, 2003

Sens en tous sens. Autour des travaux de Jean-Luc Nancy (with F. Guibal) Galilée, 2004

Le Corps de l'empreinte. Études photographiques, Kimé, 2004

100 mots pour jouir de l'érotisme, Les Empêcheurs de penser en rond/Seuil, 2004

100 mots pour 100 philosophes. De Héraclite à Derrida, Les Empêcheurs de penser en rond/Seuil, 2005

Éloge de l'inconsommable, Éditions de L'éclat, 2006

Borges. Une biographie de l'éternité, Éditions de L'éclat, 2006

Constellation de la philosophie. Badiou, Deleuze, Derrida, Foucault, Lyotard, Nancy, Rancière..., Kimé, 2007

L'œil-cerveau (with Éric Allez), Vrin, 2007

Breviary of Eternity. Between Vermeer and Spinoza, Éditions Léo Scheer, 2011

The criminal intrigue of philosophy. Read Hegel's Phenomenology of Spirit, Les Empêcheurs de penser en rond/La Découverte 2009

Plurivers. Essai sur la fin du monde, PUF, "Travaux pratiques", 2010

Deleuze, Éditions de L'éclat, 2012

Enfer de la philosophie, Éditions Léo Scheer, 2012

Derrida. Un démantèlement de l'Occident, Max Milo, 2013

Métaphysique d'Alien, (ed.), Paris, Éditions Léo Scheer, 2014

Comprendre Foucault, Paris, Max Milo, 2014

Le mal et autres passions obscures, Paris, Kimé, 2015

Derrida. Déconstruire la finitude, Paris, Ellipses, 2015

Le siècle deleuzien, Paris, Kimé, 2016

Novels :

La chambre, Éditions Léo Scheer, 2009

Morningside Park, Éditions Léo Scheer, 2011

Table of Contents

Best sellers Max Milo Editions

Hitler's banker, Jean-François Bouchard

Confessions of a forger, Éric Piedoie Le Tiec

The Koran and the flesh, Ludovic-Mohamed Zahed

Governing by fake news, Jacques Baud

Governing by chaos, Collectif

A political history of food, Paul Ariès

Mad in U.S.A.: The ravages of the "American model",
Michel Desmurget

Mondial soccer club geopolitics, Kévin Veyssière

Putin: Game master?, Jacques Braud

Treatise on the three impostors: Moses, Jesus, Muhammad,
The Spirit of Spinoza

TV Lobotomy, Michel Desmurget